GREAT
MOMENTS IN
SPORTS

RUTH ROUFF

Library Resource Center
Renton Technical College
3000 N.E. 4th Street
Renton, WA 98056

 THE TOWNSEND LIBRARY

P9-EAY-299

428.64 ROUFF 2012 c.2

Rouff, Ruth A.

Great moments in sports

GREAT MOMENTS IN SPORTS

TP THE TOWNSEND LIBRARY

For more titles in the Townsend Library,
visit our website: **www.townsendpress.com**

Copyright © 2012 by Townsend Press, Inc.
Printed in the United States of America

9 8 7 6 5 4 3 2 1

Cover illustration © 2012 by Hal Taylor

All rights reserved. Any **one** chapter
of this book may be reproduced without
the written permission of the publisher.
For permission to reproduce more than
one chapter, send requests to:

Townsend Press, Inc.
439 Kelley Drive
West Berlin, NJ 08091
permissions@townsendpress.com

ISBN-13: 978-1-59194-270-2
ISBN-10: 1-59194-270-5

Library of Congress Control Number:
2011941467

CONTENTS

The Brown Bomber Battles Hitler's Favorite Fighter

Heavyweight champion Muhammad Ali was famous for loudly proclaiming, "I am the greatest." Yet even Ali would probably agree that there was one fighter who was at least his equal, if not even greater. That man was known as the Brown Bomber—world heavyweight champion Joe Louis.

Joe Louis was not exactly a natural at boxing. As a teenager in Detroit in 1932, he was knocked down seven times in his first amateur fight. But his family was very poor, and he dreamed of making enough money to lift them all out of poverty. So he kept training and soon started winning. Noticing his raw power, two fight managers took him to see a veteran trainer, Jack Blackburn. Although Blackburn was himself black, he preferred to work with white fighters. There were two reasons for this. One was that in the 1930s it was much easier for whites to get a shot at title fights. This was partly a white reaction to black heavyweight champion Jack Johnson, the title-holder from 1908–1915. At a time when blacks were supposed to "know their place," Johnson went out of his way to anger whites. He humiliated his opponents. He loved to show off his money by spending it on flashy clothes, fast cars, and the late-night bar scene. Worst of all, he paraded around with white women on his arm. Some might say that Johnson was simply being himself. That was certainly true. But it was also true that in a deeply racist time, Johnson made it even harder for blacks who came after him to get title fights.

Another reason Blackburn was reluctant to train black fighters is that quite often, white judges wouldn't award them decisions. It seemed as if blacks would have to knock out their opponents to be declared the winner of a bout. As a result, Blackburn swore that the only blacks he would train would have to be world-beaters.

When Jack Blackburn first watched Joe Louis in the ring, he didn't see a world-beater. Twenty-year-old Louis was unpolished. His footwork was slow, and he was easily thrown off balance. He couldn't land combinations. He had a sweet personality and seemed to lack the "killer instinct" necessary to be successful in the ring. Still, Blackburn had to admit that Louis was strong. And Blackburn needed the money. So he told Louis's managers that he would train Louis even though he didn't think they would make a dime on him. To Joe he said, "It's mighty hard for a colored boy to win decisions. The dice is loaded against you. You got to knock 'em out and keep knocking 'em out to get anywhere." Reaching for the young boxer's right hand, he added, "Let your right fist be your referee. Don't ever forget that. Let that right fist there be your referee!"

Blackburn was an excellent trainer, and Joe Louis learned quickly. Soon he began building a reputation as a devastating puncher, earning him the nickname "The Brown Bomber." If there was one thing America loved, it was a great puncher, no matter what his race. Besides, boxing needed new blood. No really exciting fighter had held the heavyweight title since the glory days of Jack Dempsey in the 1920s.

When Gene Tunney defeated Dempsey and then retired in 1928, an elimination tournament was held to decide the next heavyweight champion. A German, Max Schmeling, defeated an American, Jack Sharkey, to win the title. But Schmeling's time at the top was short. In a rematch, he lost to Sharkey. Then Sharkey lost to former circus strongman Primo Carnera. After that, Carnera lost to the colorful Max Baer. Baer had lots of talent, but preferred partying to training. In 1935, a journeyman fighter named Jim Braddock upset him. On September 24, 1935, Joe Louis had his chance against Baer. In the fourth round, he knocked him down with a vicious right and a left to the jaw. Baer got to his knees, but decided not to get to his feet. After the fight, he told reporters, "I could have struggled up once more, but when I get executed, people are going to have to pay more than twenty-five dollars a seat to see it."

When Joe Louis defeated a Spanish fighter named Paulino Uzcudun, Max Schmeling was in the audience. Later, Schmeling took films of the fight back home to Germany to study them. Although Louis had knocked out Uzcudun in the fourth round, Schmeling noticed a flaw in his style. When Louis threw a jab, he brought his left hand back too low, leaving an opening for a right-hand counterpunch.

"I have discovered that Louis can be hit by a right hand," Schmeling told reporters. "I will beat him. Wait until June. You will see."

Although Max Schmeling was German, he liked America and spoke good English. As a result, many American sportswriters liked him. In fact, many white sportswriters *wanted* him to defeat Joe Louis. Remembering the stir that Jack Johnson had caused, they actually preferred a white German champion to a black American champion.

German dictator Adolf Hitler also wanted Schmeling to win. In Hitler's way of thinking, German athletes were "supermen" and the German people were the "master race." People who were not blond and blue-eyed, he believed, were weak and inferior. He looked forward to a Schmeling victory as proof that his racial views were correct.

Hitler had already begun to put these views into practice. By 1936, German Jews had already been stripped of their citizenship. Far worse treatment would soon follow. But Hitler and his Nazi followers were not only anti-Jewish; they were also anti-black. The Nazis had an unflattering name for Joe Louis. They called him "Clay Face." They thought that because he was a member of an "inferior" race, he should never be given a chance at the championship.

Like many "good Germans" who weren't members of the Nazi party, Max Schmeling went along with Hitler. Before returning to the United States, he had lunch with the German dictator and posed for news photos with him. After meeting with Hitler, Schmeling gushed to a reporter, "[that] was the most wonderful hour of my life!"

When Schmeling returned to America, he began training hard for his bout with Louis. He ran mile after mile every day in upstate New York and took countless jabs from his sparring partners. He believed that taking such punishment would prepare him to get close enough to Louis to knock him out with a terrific right hand.

Meanwhile, Joe Louis trained in Lakewood, New Jersey, but he didn't train very hard. He had fought a number of fights and had won them fairly easily. Thinking that fighting Schmeling would mean another easy victory, Louis cut down on the time he spent running, skipping rope, and punching the bags. He talked back to Jack Blackburn when the trainer told him to work harder. Some days Louis spent more time on a nearby golf course than in the boxing ring. Sportswriters who visited his training camp thought that he had gotten lazy. As one sportswriter put it, "Instead of the relentless kid fighting for his life, Joe is now a guy fighting for more money in the bank, another car, another suit, another day in the sun over Lakewood."

Still, on the day of the fight, July 19, 1936, the odds were 10–1 that Joe Louis would defeat Max Schmeling. As the fight began that night in Yankee Stadium, Louis scored with his left jab, closing Schmeling's left eye and splitting his lip.

In the second round, Schmeling landed a right that momentarily dazed Louis. Still, Louis won the first two rounds. In the third round, Louis continued to punish Schmeling with his left jab. But by the fourth round, Schmeling could time Louis's jabs. Doing so enabled Schmeling to react more quickly. When Louis came in again and threw a quick jab, the German threw a right cross over Louis's lowered left hand. The punch hit Louis squarely in the face, causing him to stagger backward. Schmeling followed, landing another right. A third right struck Louis's jaw and knocked him on his backside. This was the first time Louis had ever been knocked down as a pro.

Nazi broadcaster Arno Hellmis was joyful. "Louis is down . . . Max knocked him down! Bravo, Max! Bravo!"

At ringside, Louis's wife Marva cried, "Joe, honey, get up!" Louis staggered to his feet, dazed. He got Schmeling in a clinch to avoid further damage that round.

However, when Schmeling walked to his corner, he told his trainer, "Now I got him."

In the fifth round, all Joe Louis could do was try to avoid Schmeling. At the end of the round, Schmeling pulled his arm back to throw another right. Hearing the bell, Louis dropped his hands, and Schmeling landed a terrific right against his jaw. The punch knocked Louis senseless. His handlers had to drag him to his corner. In the sixth and seventh rounds, Schmeling continued to batter Joe Louis. Louis's mother was among those at Yankee Stadium that night. Seeing the beating her son was taking, she cried out, "My God, my God, don't let him kill my child!" A family friend led her from the stadium.

Only Louis's youth, courage, and excellent conditioning enabled him to last until the twelfth round. In that round, Schmeling's final punch sent Louis sprawling against the ropes, then down on his knees. Finally, Louis fell flat onto the canvas, rolled onto his belly, and was counted out. It took several men to carry him back to his dressing room.

Many American whites cheered for Schmeling.

"Louis is just a beaten, pitifully dejected colored boy," one wrote. Another said that Louis's nickname should be changed from the "Brown Bomber" to the "Brown Bummer." However, blacks and Jewish people didn't celebrate. To both groups, Joe Louis's defeat at the hands of Hitler's favorite fighter was a nightmare.

"I guess I fooled you guys," Schmeling told the press. Reporters called his victory the greatest upset in ring history. Hitler sent him a congratulatory telegram.

After being given smelling salts, Joe Louis woke up in his dressing room. Then he hid his badly swollen face in his hands and cried. A rumor spread that he had been drugged before the fight, but Louis quickly laid this rumor to rest.

"There was nothing wrong in my fight with Schmeling but his right hand," he told reporters.

"The myth of Joe Louis is smashed, smashed for all times," proclaimed a Nazi newspaper. Former heavyweight champion Jack Dempsey agreed. "Black fighters are never the same after a punishing loss," he said.

But Joe Louis knew that he had lost to Schmeling because he had been overconfident, not because Schmeling was the better fighter.

"I let myself down. I let a whole race of people down because I was some kind of hot s--t," he said. "I'm gonna come back."

It would take two years before Louis and Schmeling met again. During that time, Americans awakened to the threat of Hitler and Nazism. By now they knew of the concentration camps Hitler had built to get rid of so-called "undesirables." They also knew that Hitler was building up German's military might in a bid to control all of Europe. When Hitler invaded Austria in March 1938 and threatened to take over part of Czechoslovakia, it looked as if war with Germany would come soon.

On June 22, 1937, Joe Louis won the heavyweight championship by knocking out reigning champion Jim Braddock in Chicago. Blacks rejoiced at Louis's victory. However,

Louis knew the world would not really accept him as heavyweight champion until he defeated Schmeling.

In the weeks leading up to the second Louis–Schmeling fight, Joe Louis trained harder than ever before. There was no more playing golf. By now Louis had a grudge against Schmeling. He thought the German had hit him late during the fifth round of their first fight. Also, trainer Jack Blackburn had told Joe what Hitler thought of blacks.

"I don't like Schmeling because his people don't like my people," Joe Louis told the press. Together he and Blackburn worked to correct the flaw in Louis's technique that had contributed to his defeat. As the date of the fight drew closer, Louis grew more and more confident. But this time his confidence was based on solid preparation, not arrogance. He predicted that he would defeat Schmeling in the second round.

On the day of the rematch, June 22, 1938, someone handed Max Schmeling a telegram from Adolf Hitler. It read, "To the next world's champion, Max Schmeling. Wishing you every success."

Nearly 67,000 fans poured into Yankee Stadium for the fight. Nearly one hundred million people listened to it on the radio—the largest radio audience in history. In Germany, millions of people woke up at 3 a.m. to listen in and root for Schmeling. However, by now most Americans were rooting for Joe Louis. They had grown to like and admire him. Although he had defeated white opponents, he didn't gloat over the fact. Even more importantly, Americans now saw him as a champion of democracy in the face of the Nazi threat.

As the bell rang to start the fight, Joe Louis's face was taut with rage. Since he had learned the hard way that Schmeling did best when the pace of the fight was slow, Louis took the fight right to him. Moving quickly across the ring, he drove Schmeling against the ropes with a barrage of punches. And this time he kept his left hand raised after each jab. Thirty seconds into the fight, Louis hit Schmeling with a right that spun the German's head around. A few seconds later, a ferocious punch to Schmeling's side caused him to scream in pain. A reporter at ringside called the terrible cry "half human, half animal."

"How's that, Mr. Super-race?" Louis later said. Louis's punches came so fast that the eye could not follow them. Five punches to the head had Schmeling sagging against the ropes. A minute and a half into the fight, Louis knocked Schmeling to his knees with two mighty rights. As the referee rushed over to begin the count, Schmeling rose to his feet. Louis then hit the challenger with another vicious right that once more sent him to the canvas. This time Schmeling rose to his feet at the count of four.

Renton Tech Coll Library

"Louis attacks again! Why, this is madness!" wailed Nazi broadcaster Arno Hellmis. Again Louis knocked Schmeling down. By now, even some reporters were shouting, "Stop it!" Seeing the brutal beating that Schmeling was taking, his trainer, Max Machon, threw a white towel into the ring. But the referee simply picked up the towel and threw it toward the ropes. At that point, Machon threw *himself* into the ring. As Schmeling struggled to get up, the referee declared the fight over.

By now Arno Hellmis was practically crying. His German "superman" had been crushed.

This time, Americans celebrated Joe Louis's victory. A cartoon in the *Chicago Daily News* showed a plane named the Brown Bomber dropping a bomb next to Adolf Hitler. In Harlem and other black communities across America, people danced in the streets. One black sportswriter said it was like Christmas, New Year's Eve, and the Fourth of July all rolled into one.

"*Now* I feel like a champ," said Joe Louis.

As Max Schmeling retreated to Germany, Joe Louis became a national hero—the first African American to do so. Despite spending three years in the army during World War II, he defended his title 25 times and held it until he retired in 1949. No champion has held the title longer or defended it so successfully.

To this day, boxing fans spend countless hours debating who was the greater fighter: Joe

Louis or Muhammad Ali. While that dispute can never be settled, it is clear that Joe Louis helped pave the way for countless black athletes—including Ali. In so doing, he made America a more democratic place than it had ever been before.

Jackie Robinson:
Number 42 Takes the Field

As Brooklyn Dodgers first baseman Jackie Robinson was leaving his apartment to play in the first game of the 1947 baseball season, he turned to his wife Rachel. "Just in case you have trouble picking me out," he jokingly told her, "I'll be wearing number 42." Of course, he knew Rachel would have no trouble picking him out. Jackie would make history later that day by becoming the first black man to play major league baseball in fifty years. Robinson's success in integrating baseball owes a great deal to his courage. It also owes much to the foresight of the Dodgers' president and general manager, Branch Rickey.

Ever since Branch Rickey was a young man in Ohio, he believed that major league baseball should be open to all races. As coach of the Ohio Wesleyan baseball team, he had witnessed the only black player on the team, Charles Thomas, being refused a hotel room. The humiliation that Thomas suffered was something Rickey never forgot.

"I may not be able to do something about racism in every field," he later said, "but I can sure do something about it in baseball." From 1925 to 1942, Rickey had been the general manager of the St. Louis Cardinals. Although he built the Cardinals into a winner, he knew that St. Louis was too Southern a city to accept a black man playing for the team. But in 1943, Rickey became president and general manager of the Brooklyn Dodgers. He realized the time was ripe to go forward with his goal of integrating baseball. Not only would he be doing the right thing by hiring black talent; he would also be making the Dodgers winners for years to come. So he ordered his scouts to search the Negro leagues for excellent players. He wanted them to find a man who had great athletic ability and was also smart and tough enough to withstand the racism he would certainly face.

However, Rickey was not yet ready to let the world know of his plan to integrate baseball. So he announced that his scouts were looking for players for a new Negro league team, to be called the Brooklyn Brown Dodgers. As the Dodger scouts searched the Negro leagues, one man they gave high marks to was Jack Roosevelt Robinson. A star athlete at UCLA, Robinson was known as a man who stuck up for his race. Years before Rosa Parks, he had been court-martialed for refusing to move to the back of a bus while in army training in the South. During his trial, Robinson had been found not guilty and granted an honorable discharge. Now he was playing well in the Negro American League for the Kansas City Monarchs. The league was poorly run, though, and Jackie disliked the long hours spent on a bus traveling from city to city. When Dodgers scout Clyde Sukeforth told Jackie that Branch Rickey wanted him to become a Brooklyn Brown Dodger, Jackie agreed to meet with the Dodgers' president.

On August 28, 1945, Jackie Robinson entered Branch Rickey's New York office. As Robinson sat down, Rickey looked at him long and hard. Jackie looked hard right back at him.

"Do you have a girl?" Rickey finally asked Robinson. Surprised by the question, Robinson replied that he was engaged.

"Good," said Rickey. "There are times when a man needs a woman by his side." Then he came to the point. He told Robinson that he was thinking of hiring him to play not for the Brown Dodgers, but for the Brooklyn Dodgers. This "Noble Experiment," as he called it, would succeed only if Robinson could control his temper. Then Rickey began to act. He acted the part of fans that would curse Robinson because of his race, of hotel managers who would refuse to rent him a room, of pitchers who would throw at his head, and of base runners who would try to spike him with their cleats.

Robinson was amazed. "Mr. Rickey, do you want a man who's afraid to fight back?" he asked.

"I want a man with the courage not to," Rickey shot back. He convinced Robinson that only by turning the other cheek would he be able to pave the way for other blacks to enter the majors. However, after Robinson became established, he would be free to act as he saw fit. Realizing what was at stake, Robinson agreed. "I knew I had to do it for so many reasons," Jackie wrote in his autobiography. "For black youth, for my mother, for Rae [his wife Rachel], for myself. I had already begun to feel I had to do it for Branch Rickey."

In 1946, Robinson played for the Montreal Royals, the Dodgers' top minor league team. That was difficult enough, especially when the team went on the road. But when Robinson was promoted to the majors in April 1947, some members of the Brooklyn Dodgers rebelled. Many were Southerners. They had been raised to think that separation of the races was normal. Fearing what their family and friends in the South would say if they played on a team with a black man, they started a petition saying they refused to play with Robinson. When Dodgers manager Leo Durocher found out about the petition, he held a meeting.

"I'm the manager of this team," said Durocher, "and I say he plays." Durocher added that Robinson was going to put money in all their pockets by helping the team get to the World Series.

Branch Rickey also spoke to the Dodgers. Calling them one by one into his hotel room, he asked each of them if they were willing to play on an integrated team. He told them that Robinson was a great player who would help them win the pennant. Most of the players told Rickey that they were prepared to play with Robinson. However, the team's best hitter, a Southerner named Dixie Walker, wrote Rickey a letter asking to be traded. Rickey tried to trade Walker to the Pittsburgh Pirates, but he asked for too much in return, and the deal fell through.

As the 1947 season got underway, Jackie Robinson got off to a slow start. Since he knew that playing well was the key to being accepted, he may have been trying too hard. He swung at bad pitches and failed to get hits. Although most of the Dodger fans were encouraging, many of the Dodger players either ignored him or made nasty comments under their breath. Second baseman Eddie Stanky didn't mince words.

"Before I play with you, I want you to know how I feel about it," Stanky told Robinson. "I want you to know I don't like it. I want you to know I don't like *you*."

Robinson looked Stanky in the eye. "All right," he said. "That's the way I'd rather have it. Right out in the open."

Strangely enough, after Stanky had his say, he proved to be a good teammate. He knew Robinson had never played first base before and gave him excellent advice about how to play each hitter, when to shade a batter toward the foul line and when to move closer to second base.

"Stanky was gruff . . . but helpful," Robinson later said.

Thing got worse when the Philadelphia Phillies came to town. That's when the really vicious insults began. Led by manager Ben Chapman, the Phillies yelled abuse at Robinson from the visitors' dugout. Bench jockeying, as it was called, had long been a part of baseball, as each team tried to gain an edge. But the Phillies sank into the gutter to insult Robinson.

"They're waiting for you in the jungle, black boy!" they shouted. And "Hey nigger, why don't you go back to the cotton field where you belong?"

Jackie Robinson later admitted that Tuesday, April 22, 1947, was the day that "brought me nearer to cracking up than I ever had been before." As he later wrote, "For one wild and rage-crazed minute I thought, 'To hell with Mr. Rickey's noble experiment.' . . . To hell with the image of the patient black freak I was supposed to create. I could throw down my bat, stride over to that Phillies dugout, grab one of those white sons of bitches and smash his teeth in with my despised black fist. Then I could walk away from it all."

But Robinson remembered what he had promised Rickey: that he would "turn the other cheek." It was the price to be paid for making the experiment work.

In a way, the Phillies helped Robinson. They angered the Dodgers so much that for the first time, Jackie's teammates stuck up for him. Eddie Stanky screamed right back at the Phillies. "Listen, you yellow-bellied cowards," he hollered, "why don't you yell at somebody who can answer back?"

Reporters also rallied around Robinson. Walter Winchell, the most popular journalist in the country, said, "Ballplayers who don't want to be in the same ball park with Robinson don't belong in the same country with him!" Still, the pressure on Jackie continued. During April, due to a sore shoulder, he hit only .225. Rachel, who attended all the Dodgers' home games, noticed her husband tossing and turning in his sleep. She realized that Jackie's happiness depended on his batting average.

Then came a road trip to Philadelphia. In a phone call to Branch Rickey, the general manager of the Phillies, Herb Pennock, threatened to have his players boycott the game.

"We won't be able to take the field against your Brooklyn team if that boy Robinson is in uniform," Pennock told Rickey. But Commissioner Happy Chandler ordered the Phillies to play. During one game, some of the Phillies held their bats like machine guns and pretended to mow Robinson down.

Even worse, Jackie Robinson was receiving death threats in the mail. To gain support for his rookie first baseman, Branch Rickey decided to let reporters know about the threats. When people around the country learned of them, many wrote to Jackie expressing their support. One man wrote: "I happen to be a white Southerner. But I just wanted you to know that not all us Southerners are S.O.B.'s . . . I should also say that you're doing a darned fine job for all Americans." A black man wrote, "If I can raise my boy to be half the man that you are, I'll be a happy father." Meanwhile, vendors outside Ebbets Field began doing a brisk business selling "I'm for Jackie" buttons.

In May, Robinson's shoulder healed, and his batting average climbed to .299. Although he couldn't fight back, he "hurt" the opposition by performing well. Whenever he got on base, he took a large lead. Afraid that he would steal, pitchers got jumpy. Catchers called for fastballs because they were easier to handle if Robinson started running. But a steady stream of fastballs made it easier for Dodger batters to get hits. And more hits usually meant more Dodger victories.

One reporter wrote a poem about Jackie's base running:

> **Jackie's nimble,**
> **Jackie's quick,**
> **Jackie's making**
> **The turnstiles click.**

The reporter had it right: Jackie had become the biggest attraction in baseball since Babe Ruth. His killer instinct on the baseball field showed most when he stole home. As he danced back and forth between third base and home plate, he drove pitchers crazy. This daring play would become his trademark. During his career, he stole home an astonishing 19 times—placing him in the top ten all-time list for this nearly impossible feat.

By midsummer, it was clear that Jackie was carrying the team. On July 18, the Dodgers were in first place. However in August, the St. Louis Cardinals got hot and narrowed the Dodgers' lead. During the fourth game of an important series in Brooklyn, the Cardinals and Dodgers were tied in the 11th inning. When Cardinals star Enos "Country" Slaughter hit a sharp ground ball to first base, Jackie fielded the ball cleanly and stepped on first base. As he did so, he felt terrible pain shoot through the back of his right leg, above his heel. To the crowd and reporters covering the game, it seemed clear that Slaughter had intentionally spiked Robinson. Jackie was furious as he called timeout, but once more, he turned the other cheek. The umpire said nothing. Although Jackie stayed in the game, the Dodgers lost. After the game, Robinson told reporters that he thought Slaughter had intentionally spiked him. In September, the Dodgers took two out of three from the Cardinals to win the pennant. Jackie went 6-for-13 with three walks and a stolen base. It seemed the angrier he got, the better he played.

Dixie Walker was now a believer. "No other player on this club," he said, "has done more to put the Dodgers up in the race than Robinson has. He is everything Branch Rickey said he was when he came up from Montreal."

About a week later, the *Sporting News* named Jackie Robinson the 1947 Rookie of the Year. As the Dodgers returned to Brooklyn for the World Series, huge crowds awaited them. Together, Robinson and Walker assured the crowds that the Dodgers would defeat the Yankees. But they were wrong. The Yankees defeated the Dodgers in seven games. After the final game, Jackie's teammates shook his hand and congratulated him on a great season.

By now it was clear that Jackie Robinson had changed the face of baseball. In 1948 the Dodgers brought up another black man, future Hall of Fame catcher Roy Campanella. In 1949, they brought up another, pitching ace Don Newcombe. The Cleveland Indians and the New York Giants also fielded black players. By 1959, all major league teams had at least one black player. And certain teams—like the Cardinals, Red Sox, and Phillies—that had dragged their heels soon found themselves struggling to catch up with teams with black stars. Even more importantly, due to Robinson's example, more and more blacks began challenging racial barriers.

Jackie Robinson was no longer alone. And in 1949, he began fighting back. During spring training, he threatened to punch a pitcher who had almost hit him with a pitch. He argued umpires' calls and became a master bench jockey himself. No longer having to keep his emotions in check agreed with him. He led the league in batting with a .342 average, while stealing a league-leading 37 bases. Not surprisingly, he was awarded the National League's Most Valuable Player award.

Jackie Robinson played fiercely until his retirement in 1957. While he was a Dodger, the team won six pennants and one World Series. After baseball, he went on to become a successful business executive and civil rights activist. In 1962, he was elected to baseball's Hall of Fame. However, Jackie's health rapidly declined due to diabetes and heart disease. Sadly, he died of a heart attack in 1972 when he was just 53 years old.

But Jackie Robinson's legacy lives on. On April 15, 1997, Major League Baseball retired his uniform number. In honor of Robinson's remarkable achievement, no team will ever assign number 42 to one of its players. And in 2004, April 15 was designated as Jackie Robinson Day. Every year since then, on this date, all major league teams honor his memory. And on this date, players around the league wear number 42 when they take the field. They are paying tribute to the man who changed baseball, and America, for the better.

Super Bowl III:
Broadway Joe Steals the Show

Today two National Football League teams battle it out every February in the most watched sporting event in America—the Super Bowl. Yet in the mid-1960s, there were two major football leagues. One was the NFL, which had been founded in 1920. The other was the upstart

American Football League, which had been founded in 1959 by Texas oilman Lamar Hunt. In its first season, the AFL had eight teams. Not one of them was considered the equal of the best NFL teams.

"Mickey Mouse teams," some fans called the AFL teams. Yet others actually preferred watching the AFL. They liked the AFL teams' daring, wide-open style of play. In contrast to the NFL's "grind it out" style, which favored the running game, the AFL was known as a passer's league. Hotshot quarterbacks like Daryle Lamonica of the Oakland Raiders and Joe Namath of the New York Jets were not afraid to throw the long bomb, often with spectacular results. In fact, so many fans started following AFL games that NFL owners took notice. They knew that they would have to reach an agreement with the new league or risk losing even more fans.

In the 1966 season, the NFL and AFL started playing interleague championship games. There was really nothing "super" about the first two contests. In January 1967, the NFL champion Green Bay Packers defeated the AFL champion Kansas City Chiefs by a score of 35–10. In 1968, the Packers whipped the Oakland Raiders 33–14. Ho-hum. Someone's bright idea of calling the third interleague championship the "Super Bowl" seemed misguided. Although the Baltimore Colts, not the Green Bay Packers, would be representing the NFL in 1969, most fans expected the outcome to be much the same. The Colts had a record of 15–1. They had destroyed their opponents, winning ten straight games. In the NFL championship game, they had crushed the Cleveland Browns by a score of 34–0. In contrast, the Jets had narrowly defeated the Oakland Raiders 27–23 in the AFL championship game. As a result, some didn't even consider the Jets the best team in the AFL, let alone in all of pro football.

Jimmy the Greek, the most famous oddsmaker in America, picked the Colts to win Super Bowl III by 17 points. He was not alone.

"The Colts will demolish the Jets," said most experts. "The Colts are unbeatable," echoed others. In part, they based their reasoning on the fact that a number of AFL players had been cut by NFL teams. On the Jets, wide receiver Don Maynard had been cut by the New York Giants. Defensive back Johnny Sample and offensive tackle Winston Hill had both been cut by the Colts. Even the Jets' head coach, Weeb Ewbank, had been let go by the Colts in favor of football "genius" Don Shula. How could a team of rejects win the Super Bowl?

One well-known sportswriter predicted the Colts to win 43–0. The Colts agreed that they would be easy winners. They were counting on $15,000 per player—the winner's share. Some had already spent the money. But one man believed that the experts—and the Baltimore

Colts—were wrong. He was the Jets' flashy young quarterback, Joe Namath.

The scene was Miami's crowded Touchdown Club. The time was the Thursday night before Super Bowl III. All eyes were on Jets quarterback Joe Namath as he stepped to the podium to accept an award as AFL player of the year. Although few denied Namath's talent, he didn't fit the image of what a pro athlete should be. At a time when most football players wore crew cuts and cultivated a squeaky-clean image, Namath wore his dark hair long and shaggy. His football cleats were white, not black. A free-living bachelor, he had a reputation for hanging out at nightclubs in the company of beautiful women. He even wore a $5,000 mink coat. Reporters called him "Broadway Joe" because of his love of New York nightlife. Others simply called him a loudmouth playboy.

But this was Super Bowl week, and Broadway Joe's mind was strictly on business. All week, he had been hearing what a great team the Colts were and that they would destroy the Jets. And frankly, he was sick of it. But even before he could open his mouth to speak, a Colts fan shouted out, "Hey Namath, we're gonna kick your ---!"

"Whoa, wait a minute, I've got news for you," said Joe, peering through the crowd in the direction of the voice. "We're gonna win the game, I guarantee ya!"

There was a murmur in the crowd. People turned to each other and asked, "Did he just say what I think he said?" But the reporters loved it. Broadway Joe was adding some badly needed drama into what promised to be another dull game.

Baltimore coach Don Shula agreed. "He's given the players more incentive," Shula said. "Joe has made it much more interesting."

A lot of people thought Namath was crazy. Making a prediction was one thing. But guaranteeing victory? That was going too far.

"I've never heard a quarterback making remarks like he's making," said Colts defensive tackle Billy Ray Smith. "There's nothing I like to hit more than quarterbacks, and when you get a mouthy one, it makes it that much better."

Hall of Fame quarterback Norm Van Brocklin, who was now coaching the Atlanta Falcons, agreed. "On Sunday," he said, "Joe Namath will play his *first* professional football game."

What they didn't realize was that in spite of his playboy image, Joe Namath was a student of the game. He spent time with the Jets' film projector, which he called "the one-eyed monster," and he often took game film home with him. "The one-eyed monster doesn't lie," he would say.

In the two weeks leading up to the Super Bowl, Namath spent hours studying film from the Colts' games. And he liked what he saw. Far from seeing an unbeatable team, he noticed that the Colts were slower than the Jets. This lack of speed was due to the fact that the Colts were, on average, older than the Jets. In a game where plays unfold with lightning quickness, age was a definite handicap. In addition, Namath noticed that the Colts had a tendency to "telegraph"— tip off—some of their coverages. And Joe was a master at adjusting his offense at the line of scrimmage to whatever the opposing defense was doing.

"Living and studying the game in my mind gave me the smarts to smell an opponent's weakness," Namath later said. While other quarterbacks feared the Colts' blitz, Namath looked forward to it. Why not? He had a strong arm and a quicker release than anybody else in pro football. He had two great wide receivers, George Sauer, Jr., and Don Maynard. He also had two young, quick, powerful backs, Matt Snell and Emerson Boozer. These men could not only run the ball, but would also help protect him against the blitz.

Namath also had a strong opinion about Colts quarterback Earl Morrall. He thought Morrall wasn't as good as at least four other AFL quarterbacks (including himself), and didn't mind saying so. Naturally, such talk didn't sit too well with Colts coach Don Shula.

"We're proud of [Morrall]," Shula said at a press conference, the veins on his neck rising.

"Anyone who doesn't give him the credit he deserves is wrong."

Morrall was mad, too. With his crew cut and conservative personality, he was the complete opposite of Namath. "I want to beat these guys by 40," he told the Colts' placekicker, Lou Michaels. "I want to beat them bad."

But sometimes, being a heavy favorite can be a heavy burden. Maybe the Colts wanted to beat the Jets *too* badly. Maybe overconfidence made them unable to adjust when things failed to go their way. Whatever the case, the first few minutes of Super Bowl III didn't exactly go as the Colts had expected.

On the Jets' first possession, Jets fullback Matt Snell collided with the Colts' star free safety, Rick Volk, knocking him out of the game with a concussion. Since Volk had been expected to lead the blitz for the Colts, this was a big blow. However, the Jets failed to score. The Colts then got to the Jets' 19-yard line. But they came up empty when place kicker Lou Michaels missed an easy field goal. Maybe he was trying too hard. "You could almost feel the steam go out of them," Matt Snell later said.

On the Jets' next possession, Namath threw three short passes for a first down. Then, when the Colts had been lulled into stepping up on his receivers, he threw a 55-yard bomb to his flanker, Don Maynard. Unfortunately for the Jets, the ball was slightly overthrown, and Maynard, nursing a bad hamstring, couldn't catch up with it. But the Colts didn't know about Maynard's bad hamstring. They considered him more of a threat than he was and shifted their zone defense to protect against another long bomb. This move left them vulnerable to Matt Snell's power running on the left side. It also meant that Namath could take advantage of single coverage on wide receiver George Sauer, Jr.

But not right away. As the first quarter wound down, the Colts had the ball on the Jets' six-yard line. Earl Morrall threw into a crowd, the ball was tipped, and Jets defensive back Randy Beverly caught it in the end zone for a touchback. Once again, a Colts' drive came up empty.

In the second quarter, Namath handed the ball off to Matt Snell four straight times, for a total of 26 yards. After an incomplete pass to Sauer that was nearly intercepted, the Colts came with a blitz. However, Namath was a master at reading defenses.

"*Please let them blitz*," he recalled thinking. Namath evaded the charging linebacker just in time to dump the ball off to halfback Billy Mathis, who entered the Colts' territory for the first time that day. Again and again, the Jets attacked the Colts' weak side. The drive ended with Matt Snell running into the end zone behind the blocking of Colts reject Winston Hill. Jets 7, Colts 0.

Suddenly, a Colts victory no longer looked like a sure thing. Two more Colts scoring drives ended with another missed field goal and an interception by another Colts reject, Johnny Sample. But things were about to get even worse for Baltimore. On the last play of the half, Colts receiver Jimmy Orr stood wide open at the Jets' 10-yard line. He was even waving his hands. But quarterback Earl Morrall never saw him. Instead, he saw fullback Jerry Hill and threw to him. But Hill wasn't open. Jets defender Jim Hudson jumped in front of him and intercepted the pass.

"I think Morrall was overexcited," said Lou Michaels.

The second half was scarcely better for the Colts. On their first play from scrimmage, running back Tom Matte fumbled, and the Jets recovered the ball. A few plays later, Jim Turner kicked a 32-yard field goal for New York. Later in the quarter, Turner kicked another field goal, making the score 13–0. Now the crowd at Miami's Orange Bowl sensed a historic upset. Another Jets field goal in the fourth quarter made the score 16–0.

The Colts were tired and desperate, so desperate that they brought in their not-so-secret weapon, veteran quarterback Johnny Unitas. Now "Johnny U" was already a football legend, but he had missed most of the season with an arm injury. Everyone watching knew that it would take a miracle for him to pull this one out. Unitas tried his best. His first drive fell flat. On Baltimore's next possession, Unitas drove the team all the way to the Jets' 25-yard line. However, Randy Beverly intercepted *another* pass in the end zone. It was the Jets' fourth interception of the game.

Unitas did lead the Colts to one touchdown late in the fourth quarter. But it was clear that his passes lacked the zip that they once had. After the Colts recovered an onside kick, Unitas's next three passes fell incomplete, and the Jets regained possession. Although they failed to score, they had succeeded in running down the clock to eight seconds.

As darkness fell on Miami, Unitas missed two final passes. The clock ran out with the score Jets 16, Baltimore 7. The Baltimore players looked stunned. As Namath walked off the field, he held up his index finger, signaling the Jets were "number one." Not bad for a team of rejects. He and his teammates had proven their point. In beating the "unbeatable" Baltimore Colts, they had defied the experts—and had truly made the Super Bowl "super."

Ali vs. Liston:
The "Lip" Battles the "Bear"

It was the morning of February 25, 1964. The scene was a crowded weigh-in room in Convention Hall, Miami Beach, Florida. As cameras rolled and world heavyweight champion Charles "Sonny" Liston looked on in amazement, challenger Cassius Clay began acting like a wild man. His eyes bulged. Veins on his neck popped out. It took six of his corner men to prevent him from attacking Liston then and there.

"I'm ready to rumble now!" Clay screamed at Liston. "I can beat you anytime, chump! Somebody's gonna die at ringside tonight! You're scared, chump! You ain't no giant! I'm gonna eat you alive!" All this time, Drew Bundini Brown, Clay's friend and helper, was chanting, "Float like a butterfly, sting like a bee."

The doctor conducting the pre-fight physical took Clay's blood pressure. He was shocked to see that it was 200/100—dangerously high. Not knowing any other way to explain it, the doctor stated that Clay was "emotionally unbalanced and in mortal fear." In other words, he was scared to death.

As Sonny Liston watched Clay, the corners of his mouth turned down as if he had bitten into a lemon.

"Don't let everyone know what a fool you are," he advised Clay.

But Clay was hardly a fool. What Liston didn't realize was that the challenger was only pretending to go berserk, the better to get under Liston's skin. A master of psychological warfare, Clay knew that Liston was a bully who took pleasure in others' fear of him. In fact, the only thing Liston didn't know how to deal with was a crazy man. Liston's prison experience had taught him that crazy men were dangerous—because they had no fear. So here was Clay, acting insane.

Prison was only one of the things that made Liston and Clay opposites. The 24th of 25 children fathered by a tenant farmer named Tobey Liston, Sonny Liston grew up dirt-poor outside of Forrest City, Arkansas. His father had inflicted the welts he would forever carry on his back. Unable to read or write, young Liston became an armed robber and spent over two years in Missouri State Penitentiary. It was in prison that he learned to box. After prison, he fought professionally for a manager with ties to organized crime in St. Louis. In between fights, he worked as a labor goon, breaking up strikes and keeping black workers in line. After a run-in with police, Liston fled St. Louis for Philadelphia. There he was again managed by a man with mob ties. He proceeded to battle his way through the heavyweight ranks. On September 25, 1962, he knocked out champion Floyd Patterson in the first round to gain the heavyweight title. Less than a year later, he again whipped Patterson in the first round. It was a beating so brutal that many found it painful to watch.

People spoke of the silent, gloomy-looking Liston, with his huge, 14-inch fists, as "a killing machine in the ring."

In contrast, young Cassius Marcellus Clay had grown up in a middle-class family in Louisville, Kentucky. He had attended decent schools, always had enough to eat, and wore nice clothes. As a twelve-year-old, he had learned to box to get back at a bully who had stolen his bike. After winning a gold medal in the 1960 Olympics in Rome, Clay turned professional. Although growing up in the segregated South had not been a piece of cake, he had a knack for getting along with all types of people. He was handsome and friendly, charming and funny. And of course, he loved to talk. How he loved to talk!

While in Las Vegas in 1961 for a fight, Clay watched a colorful wrestler named Gorgeous George make boastful predictions about his upcoming matches in order to boost attendance. Through studying Gorgeous George, Clay realized that he could help his career by doing the same thing. It wasn't long before reporters were calling him the "Louisville Lip." Now he was predicting the round in which he would defeat Liston.

"Round eight to prove I'm great!" he taunted the champion. "A sucker and a chump! I'm gonna whip you so baaaad! You ugly bear! Chump, chump, chump! It's prophesied for me to win! I cannot be beaten!"

The boxing world had never seen anything like Cassius Clay. And this weigh-in performance took his outrageous behavior to a whole new level. Shaking his head in disgust, Miami boxing commissioner Morris Klein fined Clay $2,500 for his antics.

Sonny Liston, the "big ugly bear," only scowled back at Clay. Most of the people who followed boxing thought he would demolish the challenger.

"The biggest thing about Clay is his mouth," they agreed. For one thing, for all Clay's boasting, he hadn't shown the knockout punch that Liston had. While Clay was known mostly for his stinging jab, people said that Liston hit speed bags so hard that he tore them from their hinges.

"Clay is a charmer when it comes to popping off," said one boxing expert. "But he doesn't know the trouble he'll see when Sonny starts working him over with malice aforethought to do a butchery job on his pretty face."

Comedian Jackie Gleason made a joke of Clay's chances. "Clay should last about 18 seconds, and that includes the three seconds he brings into the ring with him."

Former world heavyweight champion Joe Louis joined the crowd in Liston's corner. "He [Clay] has got to be joking. I wouldn't give a nickel for his chances."

In Sonny Liston's 36 professional fights, he had won 25 by knockouts . . . many in the early rounds. Clay had won all his fights, but not in the dominating way that Liston had. In fact, most boxing experts believed Clay did everything wrong in the ring. They said he held his hands too low and that he danced around in the ring because he couldn't take a punch. They predicted that Liston would catch him and clobber him. In addition, Clay had fought only 19 professional matches. They thought he was too inexperienced to go up against a seasoned fighter like Liston. Small wonder that on the day of the fight, the odds were 7–1 in Liston's favor.

Sonny Liston might have believed he was invincible too.

"I don't know what I'm training so hard for—this kid ain't gonna last one round," he told the reporters who flocked to his training camp at the Surfside Community Center. Actually, though, Liston *didn't* train hard. He had an assistant throw a medicine ball against his rock-hard stomach. He jumped rope to a slow blues number, "Night Train." Sometimes he would beat up a little on his sparring partners—nothing too tiring. In his mind, Clay was a fresh kid, a loudmouth punk who needed to be taught a lesson.

However, the "lesson" didn't turn out quite the way Liston had planned.

As the bell for Round 1 rang in Miami Beach, Sonny Liston came out almost at a run. It was as if he couldn't wait to make Clay pay for all the insults the challenger had thrown at him. But Clay easily danced out of reach of Liston's punches, backpedaling, bobbing, and weaving.

"Man, he meant to kill me," Clay later said. "I just kept running, watching his eyes. Liston's eyes tip you when he's about to throw a heavy punch."

As the seconds ticked off, Liston caught Clay with blows to the body, but could not land a punch to his head. Towards the end of the round, Clay came back with some blows of his own, including a volley of lefts and rights that tattooed Liston's face. Snorting in rage, Liston lunged forward to attack his enemy, but once more Clay danced away as the bell rang, ending the round.

"I remember I got back to my corner thinking, 'He was supposed to kill me.' Well, I'm still alive," Clay said afterward.

The press, too, was beginning to sense that something amazing was about to happen. After all, Clay had done what many a man before him had been unable to do . . . survive a round with Liston.

In the second round, Liston again came out punching. But again Clay danced and weaved, dodging Liston's deadly body blows. Clay was a hit-and-run artist, snapping lightning-fast jabs at Liston's head and then dancing out of reach. One punch opened up a small cut over Liston's cheekbone. As Clay reached in to hit that target, Liston hit Clay with his hardest punch of the fight, a left to Clay's jaw. But though the punch rocked Clay, it did not stop him. Round 3 was all Clay: Liston simply couldn't keep up with the younger man, whose knifing, twisting punches decorated the champ's face with cuts and bruises.

What occurred next is the stuff of legend. To this day, no one is sure what happened. All we know is that when Cassius Clay returned to his corner at the end of Round 4, he told his trainer, Angelo Dundee, that there was something in his eyes.

"Cut the gloves off!" Clay demanded. "I can't see!"

Some unknown substance had gotten into the fighter's eyes. Perhaps it was a chemical that had been applied to close Liston's cut. Perhaps someone in Liston's corner had "doctored" Liston's gloves with something he knew would blind Clay. The Muslims in Clay's corner were growing angry. They suspected that Dundee, a white man, had sabotaged their fighter's chances. But when Dundee reached into the bucket and splashed some of the water he had used to clear Clay's eyes into his own eyes, the Muslims knew that Dundee was innocent.

As Dundee pushed his fighter back into the ring, he shouted, "You can't quit now. This is the big one, Daddy! Run!"

Half blind, Clay danced away from the dim figure of Liston as if his life depended on it.

"Keep away from him, Cass!" screamed Dundee over the roar of the crowd. "Just keep away from him!"

Once again, Clay's blinding speed and left jab saved him from the full effects of Liston's power. By the end of the round, Clay's eyes were clearing. In Round 6, he beat Liston without mercy, hitting him with a combination of lefts and rights, doubling him up in pain. By now, Liston's face was horribly swollen. Blood was steaming from the cut under his eye and from his nose. Someone later said that he looked as if he had aged ten years in three minutes.

Clay later recalled, "I remember thinking something like 'Yeah, you old sucker. You try to be so big and bad!' He was gone. He knew he couldn't last."

As the warning ten-second buzzer sounded for Round 7, Clay rose to his feet. But as he watched in amazement, Liston spat out his mouthpiece. He was tired and beaten. He had injured his arm during the fight. Liston knew that if he stayed in the ring, he would get knocked out. Later, it was learned that he had torn the tendon of his left bicep.

Clay was probably the first to realize that Liston had quit. He raised both arms in triumph and began furiously dancing around the ring.

"I'm king! I'm the greatest!" he screamed before a stunned audience. In a moment, Bundini Brown jumped into the ring to hug Clay, lifting him off the ground. A huge grin spread across Angelo Dundee's face as he, too, joined his fighter in the ring.

"Eat! Eat! Eat your words!" Clay shouted at the press. "I'm so great! I don't have a mark on my face and I upset Sonny Liston and I just turned 22 years old . . . I shook up the world! I shook up the world! I shook up the world!"

One day later, Cassius Clay would again shake up the world when he formally announced that he had joined the Nation of Islam, a Black Muslim group that preached racial separation. In doing so, he renounced his "slave name" of Cassius Clay and stated that from now on he would be known as Muhammad Ali. Many white people were outraged. They didn't understand Ali's choice of religion. They felt he was accusing all whites of being racists. They didn't understand that, to Ali, becoming a Muslim was more an expression of black pride than one of hostility toward whites.

In the years to come, Muhammad Ali would continue to shock and amaze the world. Meanwhile, Sonny Liston's life went rapidly downhill. In a rematch held in Lewiston, Maine, in 1965, Ali knocked Liston out in the first round. Some people thought the fight had been fixed, that Liston had "taken a dive" on orders from the Mafia. Although Sonny Liston continued to fight, he started drinking heavily. On January 5, 1971, he was found dead in his Las Vegas home. Officially, the cause of death was heart failure. However, an autopsy revealed traces of narcotics in his system. This finding led police to suspect that he had died of a drug overdose. It was a sad and lonely ending for the former world champion.

Roberto Clemente:
A Legend On and Off the Field

In the past thirty years or so, many of the biggest names in baseball have been Latino. However, when Roberto Clemente joined the Pittsburgh Pirates in 1955, the situation was very different. Not only was he one of only two Spanish-speaking players on the team; he was also one of the few blacks.

"I am between worlds," he once told a sportswriter, "so anything I do will reflect on me because I am black . . . will reflect on me because I am Puerto Rican." Although Clemente had been raised never to dislike a person because of the color of his skin, he quickly found out that in the United States, color was a very big deal. In spring training at Fort Myers, Florida, he learned that he could neither room nor eat with his white teammates. Nor could he swim at the same beaches and pools. Since segregation was still the rule in the South, life there for black ballplayers was like being in jail. The situation in Fort Myers angered Clemente, but there was little he could do about it.

Things improved somewhat when the Pirates headed north to begin the regular season. In Pittsburgh, most hotels and restaurants were open to Clemente. The Latino population of Pittsburgh was tiny, however, and there were almost no Puerto Ricans in the city. Clemente had only one Latino teammate. As a result, he was lonely and homesick.

To make matters worse, Roberto's relationship with white sportswriters got off to a rocky start. Since the writers knew so little about Latinos, they stereotyped him as a hot-tempered showoff. They also quoted Clemente in broken English, making him sound stupid. Not surprisingly, Roberto took offense. "I never in my life started a sentence with 'me,'" he declared.

In contrast, the same sportswriters wrote favorably of the other Pirates. These players were more like themselves—hard-drinking white guys who spoke English without a Spanish accent.

Despite unfair treatment by the press, Clemente played hard. Still, he was not an overnight sensation. In his rookie season, he batted only .255. From 1956 to 1960, he hit over .300 only one time. His slow start was partly the result of injuries. In 1954, a speeding car struck Clemente's car. The crash badly injured Roberto's spine and led to constant back pain for the rest of his career. Later on, he developed arthritis in his neck as a result of the crash. That was why he would twist his neck back and forth as he stepped into the batter's box. He was getting the kinks out.

In addition to *having* physical problems, Clemente liked to *talk* about them. This was at a time when most men were expected to be the "strong, silent type." Pirates manager Danny Murtaugh thought Clemente was too sensitive. He accused him of being unwilling to play through pain. Reporters went further. They said Clemente was a hypochondriac—someone whose ailments are imaginary.

On the brighter side, many Pittsburgh fans adored Roberto from the beginning. They appreciated his intense style of play. Pirates broadcaster Bob Prince did too. When Clemente stepped to the plate, Prince would lead the fans in chanting, "*Arriba! Arriba!*"—the Spanish equivalent of "Let's go!"

Roberto Clemente's breakout year came in 1960. A slashing line-drive hitter, he batted .314 with 94 runs batted in and 16 home runs. Since Forbes Field had a huge outfield, hitting 16 home runs was an accomplishment. Clemente's great offense and defense helped lead the Pirates into the World Series. In the Series, the Pirates faced the powerful New York Yankees, who boasted such sluggers as Mickey Mantle and Yogi Berra. Clemente did his part for the Pirates by hitting safely in all seven games. He showed off his rocket arm and made several outstanding catches. In Game 5, he hit a key single that knocked in a run. And in Game 7, in the bottom of the eighth with two out, he beat out an infield hit and narrowed the Yankees' lead to one run. One inning later, Bill Mazeroski hit a dramatic home run to win the Series for the Pirates. During the post-game celebration, Clemente sat quietly as his teammates poured champagne on each other. Few reporters paid much attention to him. However, as he left Forbes Field, adoring fans mobbed him. Earlier, they had voted him the most popular Pirate.

During the 1960 season, Clemente had led the Pirates in runs batted in and total bases. He had finished second in batting average and was clearly the best right fielder in the league. After returning to Puerto Rico, he waited for the baseball writers to vote for the National League's Most Valuable Player. He thought he had a good shot. However, his teammate, shortstop Dick Groat, won the award. Clemente could accept Groat's victory. Harder to accept was finishing in 8th place in the MVP voting. This lack of respect angered Clemente. It also fueled his desire to prove the writers wrong.

In the next few seasons, Roberto Clemente became one of the best hitters in baseball. In 1961, he hit .351 and won his first batting championship. He also won the batting title in 1964, 1965, and 1967. Throughout the 1960s, he had the highest batting average of any player in the major leagues. In 1966, he was finally named Most Valuable Player. And as he became a star, he became a mentor for the growing number of Latinos on the club. His personal life became happier too, as he wed a beautiful young Puerto Rican woman named Vera Zabala. The couple soon had three sons. They lived in a large, modern home on a hilltop outside of San Juan. But even though Roberto was a star, it still bothered him that players on New York or California teams got much more recognition than he did. This situation would change in 1971, when Clemente once again led the Pirates into the World Series.

By 1971, most baseball fans knew that Clemente was one of the best players in the game. Yet many had never seen him in action.

When Pittsburgh defeated the Giants in the National League Championship Series, the stage was set for him to shine before millions. The Pirates would face the heavily favored Baltimore Orioles in the World Series. The Orioles boasted not one but four twenty-game winners, as well as future Hall of Famers Frank Robinson and Brooks Robinson.

After Baltimore took the first two games of the series in Baltimore, one reporter wrote, "The Pirates should ask where they go to surrender." However, Roberto Clemente was confident. He had already gotten hits in the first two games. In addition, he had made a laser-like throw from deep right field to nearly nail an Orioles' runner at third base. In fact, many fans still consider that throw to be the greatest play of the entire series. Still, the Orioles won the game, 11–3. Clemente told his teammates, "Don't worry about it. We're going to Pittsburgh, and that's our ballpark."

True enough, the Pirates struck back in Game Three. Right-hander Steve Blass pitched brilliantly, and first baseman Bob Robertson hit a three-run home run. Roberto got another two hits and was safe on an error.

In Game Four, Clemente got another three hits as the Pirates won, 4–3. By now, the organist at Three Rivers Stadium was playing "Jesus Christ Superstar" every time Clemente came to bat. In addition, the sports writers were now on Clemente's side. Dick Young of the *New York*

Daily News wrote, "The best damn ballplayer in the World Series, maybe in the whole world, is Roberto Clemente."

The Pirates were also victorious in Game Five as Clemente singled and knocked in a key run. When it became clear that Clemente was putting on an unforgettable show, another reporter gushed, "It's about time 60 million people got in on a legend and not just Toughtown, U.S.A."

In Game Six, Clemente hit a first-inning triple and a third-inning home run. In the top of the ninth, he made a perfect throw to keep an Orioles base runner from scoring from first on a double. However, Baltimore went on to win in extra innings by a score of 3–2.

Now everything came down to Game Seven at Baltimore's Memorial Stadium. Again Clemente encouraged his teammates. "Don't worry," he told them. "We are gonna win this game. No problem."

While Steve Blass again took the mound for the Pirates, veteran Mike Cuellar pitched for the O's. Cuellar had gone 20–9 in 1971 and had lots of post-season experience. By the fourth inning, he had retired 11 straight Pirates. But when he threw Clemente a curveball over the outside part of the plate, the Pirate star reached out and smacked it into the bleachers. Clemente must have been particularly pleased to get this home run off Cuellar. He had managed the Orioles pitcher in winter ball in Puerto Rico. Cuellar had left the team because he didn't like Roberto's style of managing.

Steve Blass continued to mow down the Orioles with his outstanding slider. After Pittsburgh scored another run in the top of the eighth, the Orioles scored one run in the bottom of the eighth. However, Blass retired the side in the ninth, and the Pirates won the World Series.

This time, reporters surrounded Roberto Clemente. This time, he got all the credit anyone could possibly want. His incredible .414 batting average and brilliant fielding earned him the *Sport Magazine* Award as the outstanding player of the Series.

"Now people in the whole world know the way I play—not that I am a hypochondriac—that I am a .300 hitter," he said.

In the offseason, Roberto's thoughts turned to helping others. Throughout his career, he had often visited sick children in hospitals throughout the U.S. He had also done a good deal of charity work in Puerto Rico. Now he planned to create a "sports city" for the needy children of Puerto Rico. The complex would be made up of baseball fields, a swimming pool, and basketball and tennis courts. Children who attended would receive high-quality coaching in these sports. That winter he began trying to obtain the $2.5 million needed for the project. He seriously considered retiring but decided to play another year. It was a good decision. In his final regular-season batting appearance of 1972, he smacked a double. It was the 3,000th hit of his career.

On December 23, 1972, a terrible earthquake struck Managua, Nicaragua, killing thousands. A month earlier, Clemente and Vera had gone with the Puerto Rican team to the world amateur baseball tournament in Nicaragua. In Managua, he had met many fine people. Worried about what had become of them, he began organizing a drive for relief supplies. A few days later, he learned that thieves were stealing supplies that had already been sent. Outraged, he decided to charter a plane and deliver the supplies himself.

"No one will dare steal supplies from me," Clemente said. But the plane he chartered was old and in poor condition. Its owner had often been in trouble for ignoring safety regulations. The pilot had so many violations that he was in danger of losing his license. Roberto Clemente knew none of this.

On the night of December 31st, Clemente climbed aboard the overloaded plane. It took off and barely cleared the palm trees at the edge of the airport. A minute or so later, one of the engines caught fire. The plane crashed into the sea. Despite the efforts of search teams, Roberto's body was never found.

"If you have the chance to help others, and don't, you are wasting your time on the earth," Roberto Clemente said a year before his death. Clearly, Clemente had made the most of his time on earth. On March 20, 1973, he became the first Latino voted into the National Baseball Hall of Fame. Normally, baseball players cannot be voted on until five years after they retire. However, this rule was waived for Clemente because of his hero status. In 1974, his wife Vera carried on his dream of helping the children of Puerto Rico by opening the Roberto Clemente Sports City.

Each year Major League Baseball honors a ballplayer with the Roberto Clemente Award. It is given to the player who excels on the field and who also best demonstrates Roberto Clemente's quality of compassion for others.

In all these ways, Roberto's spirit lives on.

The Immaculate Reception:
The Greatest Touchdown
in NFL History

As the 1970s began, things were not looking great for the Pittsburgh Steelers. For most of their 37-year history, the Steelers had ranked near the bottom of the NFL standings. Needless to say, they had never won a playoff game. In 1968, they had won two games, lost eleven, and tied one. In 1969, they were even worse, winning one game and losing thirteen. "Same old Steelers," Pittsburgh fans sighed.

But then first-year head coach Chuck Noll began drafting players that would turn the Steelers around. With the fourth overall pick in 1969, he chose a little-known defensive tackle from North Texas State named Joe Greene. Although some Steelers fans questioned this selection, "Mean" Joe Greene would soon gain a reputation as being impossible to block. In fact, some experts have called Greene *the* football player of the 1970s.

In 1970, Noll used the number-one pick in the draft to select a rifle-armed quarterback from Louisiana Tech named Terry Bradshaw. Some Steelers fans saw Bradshaw as the answer to their prayers. Others thought the Steelers had wasted their pick. No one denied that Bradshaw could throw. But Louisiana Tech was a small school. As a result, Bradshaw had never played against powerhouses like the University of Alabama, Florida, or LSU. In 1970, as the Steelers' first-string quarterback, he got off to a terrible start. Unused to reading defenses, he threw twenty-four interceptions and only six touchdown passes. In addition, he completed only 38.1 percent of his passes. Not surprisingly, Coach Noll benched him after the Steelers lost their first three games. The long-suffering Pittsburgh fans booed him without mercy. Reporters called him a "dumb hick."

"There was no way I was ready to play pro

football," Bradshaw later admitted. "Emotionally, physically, I just wasn't ready." But Bradshaw slowly improved, and Noll kept drafting talented players to support him. In 1970, he drafted Southern University cornerback Mel Blount. In 1971, Penn State linebacker Jack Ham became a Steeler. In 1972, Noll drafted another Penn State standout: running back Franco Harris. All of these players were destined to make the Pro Football Hall of Fame. They would also transform the lowly Steelers into one of the most successful teams in all of pro sports.

The turning point for the Steelers turned out to be a play so remarkable that it was given its own name. The name it received is actually a play on words: specifically, the name of the Roman Catholic belief that Jesus was born without sin—in other words, conceived immaculately. Fittingly, it was a die-hard Pittsburgh Steelers fan named Michael Ord who coined the name: "The Immaculate Reception."

NFL Films has called the Immaculate Reception the greatest touchdown in pro football history. It took place when the Oakland Raiders met the Pittsburgh Steelers one drizzly afternoon in a 1972 AFC playoff semifinal. Unlike the lowly Steelers, the Oakland Raiders had been a powerhouse throughout most of the 1960s. Led by lone-wolf owner Al Davis and football wizard John Madden, they had a reputation for playing hard and dirty. In fact, many considered them as lawless as their "Raider" namesakes. Now, on December 23, 1972, at Pittsburgh's Three Rivers Stadium, they were battling it out against the Steelers. As could be expected with two great defensive teams, the game was hard-hitting and low-scoring. Pittsburgh's "Steel Curtain" defense had pretty much shut down the Raiders' offense all afternoon. But with 1:13 left in the fourth quarter, Raiders' backup quarterback Ken Stabler scrambled 30 yards down the sideline into the end zone. That made the score Raiders 7, Pittsburgh 6.

When Pittsburgh got the ball back, Terry Bradshaw quickly threw three straight incompletions. Now, on fourth down, with 22 seconds left to play, and the ball on the Steelers' own 40-yard line, Bradshaw barked out, "66 Option." This was to be a pass play over the middle that would put Pittsburgh kicker Roy Gerela in position to kick a field goal.

It didn't turn out that way. In fact, what followed next had to be seen to be believed.

As Bradshaw took the snap, he dropped back, searching for his intended receiver, rookie Barry Pearson. Just then, two Raiders crashed through the Pittsburgh offensive line. This pressure caused Bradshaw to scramble out of the pocket and to his right. A Raiders defender nearly tackled him. Then Bradshaw saw his secondary receiver, John "Frenchy" Fuqua, getting open. Realizing he was about to get hit, Bradshaw braced and threw a bullet to Fuqua. But Raiders safety Jack Tatum, who had been covering Pearson, saw that Fuqua was Bradshaw's target. He rushed over to break up the pass.

Now, Tatum already had a fearsome reputation. In fact, his brutal hits had earned him the nickname "Assassin." At the same time the ball arrived, Tatum shot a wicked right forearm against Fuqua's helmet, flattening him. As Tatum and Fuqua collided, the ball bounced off one or both of them and flew backward eight yards. Steelers running back Franco Harris spotted the ball in the air. Racing forward, he reached down and caught it a second before it hit the ground. Then he galloped 42 yards into the end zone, strong-arming Raiders defender Jimmy Warren along the way.

"I don't recollect seeing the ball at all," said Harris. "I knew Brad threw it, and just from my training at Penn State, I just went toward where I thought it was going. Before I knew it, I had the ball. It was just a blur."

Frenchy Fuqua saw the play from another angle.

"I was lying on the ground looking at Tatum," he said. "The first thing I saw after the collision was a smile on his face from ear to ear. And then, like in slow motion, I'm not kidding, I saw that smile turn to a frown. That's the way it really looked. I saw a smile, over-excitement, and joy just melt away. And I got a glimpse of Franco as he went by."

Jack Tatum recalled the play a bit differently. "After I hit Frenchy, I thought the game was over," he said. "I didn't see Franco catch the ball. I thought, "He's sure in a hurry to get to the locker room."

Meanwhile, Terry Bradshaw, who had been tackled by an Oakland defender, was also lying on the ground. When the crowd cheered, Bradshaw thought he had completed the pass to his receiver for a touchdown.

"Damn," he told himself, "you truly are amazing. You put that baby right in there." It was only after Bradshaw got to the sideline that he learned that the pass meant for Fuqua had been taken into the end zone by Harris.

As the Steelers' fans rejoiced, Jack Tatum protested. "Tell them you touched it. Tell them you touched it," he cried to Frenchy Fuqua. But Fuqua wasn't about to tell them anything of the kind. At that time, the NFL rules prevented an offensive player from deflecting a ball to his teammate. But if an Oakland Raider had touched the ball before it got to Harris, the play would be legal.

Even the officials were a little confused. Since instant replay was not yet being used to review plays, they had no video to fall back on. Although back judge Adrian Burk signaled that the play was a touchdown, the other officials did not make any signal. When the officials got together, Burk and umpire Pat Harder said they thought that the play was a touchdown because both Tatum and Fuqua had touched the ball. Three other officials said that they were not in a position to rule. Referee Fred Swearingen then called the press box to reach the NFL's supervisor of officials, Art McNally.

"Two of my men say that opposing players touched the ball, Fuqua and Tatum," said Swearingen.

"Everything's fine then. Go ahead," replied McNally.

Swearingen then went back onto the field and signaled a touchdown.

John Madden was furious. He argued that the touchdown shouldn't count because the ball had hit Fuqua and not Tatum. Bradshaw looked over and saw him.

"That was John Madden," Bradshaw later joked, "always trying to teach people about football."

But no matter how much Madden protested, the call would stand.

Years later, people are still arguing about the play. Raiders fans claim that the officials were so afraid of the hometown crowd that they ruled Harris's illegal catch legal. To this day, they refer to the play as "the Immaculate *Deception*." On the other hand, a scientist who had studied the play had a different opinion. He decided that the ball had bounced too fast and too far backward for it to have glanced off Fuqua, who was rushing away from the pass. Only by hitting a player rushing *toward* the pass—like Tatum—could the ball have caromed back so far and so fast.

Pittsburgh sportscaster Myron Cope said he reviewed film taken by local Pittsburgh TV station WTAE.

"I ran the film through a device called a viewer, slowly cranking the handle that allowed me to watch the film frame by frame, again and again, at a snail's pace," Cope said. "No question about it: Bradshaw's pass struck Tatum squarely on his right shoulder. I mean, I saw it."

In 1998, during halftime of the AFC championship game, NBC replayed a clip from its original 1972 broadcast. This clip showed the play from a different angle than the NFL film clip that is usually shown. One writer for the *New York Daily News* wrote, "NBC's replay showed the ball clearly hit one and only one man: Oakland defensive back Jack Tatum."

What does Frenchy Fuqua say about who was hit by the ball? He doesn't. He says he prefers to keep quiet. Others suggest that he simply doesn't know. After all, he was getting drilled by Jack Tatum at the time.

For his part, Jack Tatum wrote in his autobiography that he couldn't honestly say if the ball hit him.

Today, viewers can watch video clips of the

play on **Youtube.com**. A slow-motion replay suggests that the officials got it right—that the football *did* bounce off Jack Tatum's shoulder pad and into the hands of Franco Harris. Still, it's difficult to be 100 percent certain.

What *is* certain is that the play marked a turning point for the Pittsburgh Steelers' franchise. Although the Steelers narrowly lost to the Miami Dolphins in the AFC championship game, their incredible victory over the Raiders gave them a big boost of confidence. Led by its "dumb hick" quarterback, Terry Bradshaw, the team would go on to win four Super Bowls within ten years. So far, the Pittsburgh Steelers and the San Francisco 49ers are the only NFL teams to have accomplished that feat.

Ali vs. Foreman:
The Rumble in the Jungle

On April 28, 1967, heavyweight champion Muhammad Ali refused to be drafted into the United States Army. His refusal cost him dearly. His boxing license was revoked. His championship title was stripped from him. He did not fight for three years. Since he was then in his mid-twenties, these were probably the best years in his boxing life. But as a minister of the Nation of Islam, Ali felt the Vietnam War was unjust.

"I ain't got no quarrel with them Viet Cong. They never called me names," he said.

Many called Ali a traitor to his country. But as opposition to the war grew, others began to side with him. In 1970, as his case worked its way through the court system, he was permitted to fight again. He defeated two hard-hitting competitors: Jerry Quarry and Oscar Bonavena. On March 8, 1971, he challenged champion Joe Frazier and lost in 15 rounds. It was his first professional defeat. When Ali lost again, to Ken Norton in 1973, people thought that perhaps he would never regain the championship. But in a rematch, Ali defeated Norton. Then in January, 1974, he defeated Joe Frazier, who had by this time lost his title to George Foreman. Finally, the stage was set for another title fight. It would take place October 30, 1974 in the central African nation of Zaire (now called the Democratic Republic of Congo).

In some ways, the reigning heavyweight champion, George Foreman, was a lot like Sonny Liston. Both were amazingly powerful men who seemed to enjoy intimidating others. Both had grown up poor. As a teenager growing up in Houston, Texas, Foreman was often in trouble with the law. But unlike Liston, Foreman did not go to prison. Instead, he joined the Job Corps and took up boxing. In 1968, he won a boxing gold medal at the Summer Olympics in Mexico City.

The late 1960s was a time of deep division in American life. While many supported the Vietnam War, others, like Ali, did not. Increasingly, young black men were questioning why they should have to fight in Vietnam when black people were still not being treated fairly at home. Social protest spilled over into sports. In 1968, two black athletes had given the black power salute while receiving their Olympic medals, but George Foreman had not. Instead, he had waved a small American flag. Foreman's action angered Muhammad Ali. Since the United States government was punishing him for refusing to fight in Vietnam, he was in no mood to see another black man wave the American flag. He vowed to teach Foreman a lesson—if he ever got the chance.

Now, six years later, Ali's chance had come. But could he defeat Foreman? The new champion's record stood at 40–0, with 37 knockouts. His eight most recent bouts had ended in the first or second round. In his battle with Joe Frazier, Foreman had decked the smaller man six times in less than five minutes. The fight had been stopped in the second round. In contrast, it had taken Ali 15 rounds to win a decision over Frazier.

One sportswriter wrote, "George Foreman might be the heaviest puncher in the history of the heavyweight division." Visitors to his training camp reported seeing his sledgehammer punches nearly crush the heavy bag in two. Of course, Ali also hit the heavy bag. But his blows seemed feather-light compared to Foreman's.

George Foreman said simply, "My opponents don't worry about losing. They worry about getting hurt."

Now, in Zaire, the stage was set for what most saw as another lopsided contest. Only this time, George Foreman, not Sonny Liston, was the odds-on favorite to defeat Muhammad Ali.

Of course, Ali did not see things the way others saw them. He never did.

After setting up his training camp, Ali went to work winning over the local people and entertaining the press. Just as he had labeled Sonny Liston the "big ugly bear," he had a label for Foreman.

"George Foreman is nothing but a big mummy," he announced. "He moves like a slow mummy, and there ain't no mummy gonna whup the great Muhammad Ali."

When someone pointed out how hard Foreman hit, Ali replied, "Hitting power don't mean nothing if you can't find nothing to hit."

At first, the fight was set for late September. However, when Foreman's sparring partner accidentally cut him above the eye with an elbow, it had to be postponed. This month-long delay worked to Ali's favor. Unlike Foreman, he seemed to draw strength from the people who flocked to see him.

"This is my country," he told the Zairians. By that, he meant that he was proud of his African roots. He went out of his way to praise his hosts.

"I used to think Africans were savages," he said, "But now that I'm here, I've learned that many Africans are wiser than we are."

On the other hand, George Foreman didn't bother to meet the people of Zaire. In fact, he gave the impression that he didn't want to talk to anyone. He rarely spoke to reporters, which made it hard for them to write positive stories about him. When he did talk, he was rude and short-tempered. He seldom ventured out of his air-conditioned hotel room. And when he did, he took his $25,000 prize German shepherd with him. The Zairians took one look at the dog and frowned. It reminded them of the bad old days when Zaire had been controlled by Belgium. Back then, white policemen had used such dogs to keep them in line.

Rumors started circulating that Foreman was going stir-crazy. Although the rumors were probably exaggerated, he was certainly not enjoying Zaire the way Ali was.

Finally the night of the fight, October 30,

rolled around. Since the fight was being telecast live to an American prime-time audience, it was scheduled to begin at 4 a.m. in Zaire. One billion people would be watching. Sixty thousand people were in the stadium. As Ali entered his dressing room shortly before ring time, he noticed that all of his followers looked worried. Before Ali had lost to Joe Frazier and Ken Norton, they had thought he couldn't be beaten. Now they weren't so sure.

Ali took one look at them. "Everybody scared?" he playfully asked. "This ain't nothing but another day in the dramatic life of Muhammad Ali . . . Let's rumble in the jungle!"

It was 85 degrees and very humid when the two fighters took their corners. Overhead, powerful TV lights made the ring even hotter. As the bell rang to begin Round 1, the crowd expected to see the Ali of old, dancing and backpedaling out of harm's way. After all, Ali's motto had always been, "Float like a butterfly and sting like a bee."

But ten years had passed since Muhammad Ali had become heavyweight champion. During the first round, he surprised George Foreman by taking the fight to him—hitting him with a straight right to the head. Throughout much of the first round, he was the Ali of old—dazzling with his footwork and lightning-fast punches.

But in the second round, Ali did something that amazed even those closest to him. Rather than dance out of Foreman's reach, he headed toward the ropes. Planting his feet firmly, he put his hands and arms up to cover his face and body, and then let Foreman punch away.

"I won't kid you," Ali's trainer Angelo Dundee later said, "When he went to the ropes, I felt sick. The way I saw things happening was Ali dancing for five or six rounds . . . Everything we planned was built around not getting hit."

Now, before everyone's eyes, Ali was practically inviting George Foreman to bomb away at him. Why did Ali suddenly change his strategy?

Looking back on the fight, Ali said, "I didn't really plan what happened that night. But when a fighter gets in the ring, he has to adjust according to the conditions he faces. Against George, the ring was slow . . . I knew I couldn't keep dancing, because by the middle of the fight I'd be really tired, and George would get me."

So, starting in the second round, Ali gave George Foreman what Foreman *thought* he wanted. It was a risky strategy. If one of Foreman's thunderous blows got through to Ali's head, he would be knocked out cold. It was a strategy that only Ali, with his amazing ability to block punches, could make work. It didn't hurt, either, that the ropes were a little loose. Their slackness allowed Ali to lean back against them, his head a few inches out of Foreman's reach.

Still, when Ali went to his corner at the end of Round 2, his cornermen all said the same thing: "Stay off the ropes, Ali, he's going to kill you!"

But Ali wouldn't listen. "I know what I'm doing," he coolly told them.

Round 3 was almost a repeat of Round 2. Again Muhammad Ali went to the ropes. Again George Foreman eagerly battered away at him. Those in Foreman's corner were delighted. Their whole strategy had been for Foreman to somehow get Ali against the ropes and pound him there. Now, Ali was doing just as they had wished. Oh, Ali threw some stinging punches at Foreman's head, but the "Mummy" didn't let them stop him. He was still looking to land that one knockout punch.

Former light-heavyweight champion Archie Moore was standing in George Foreman's corner. "I was praying, and in great sincerity, that George wouldn't kill Ali," he later said. "I really felt that was a possibility."

Meanwhile, Ali was talking to Foreman. "Hit harder!" he said, "Show me something, George. That don't hurt. I thought you were supposed to be bad."

Several of Foreman's punches rocked Ali, but he refused to fall.

"I went out and hit Muhammad with the hardest shot to the body I ever delivered to any opponent. Anybody else in the world would have crumbled," George Foreman later said.

But Ali *didn't* crumble. Then, as the rounds wore on, Foreman's punches got slower and less powerful. They were big, looping lefts and rights that lacked the speed and crispness of Ali's punches. And because Foreman didn't move his head when he boxed, it was easy for Ali to hit him with lightning-quick combinations. For every punch Foreman landed, Ali landed five.

In the sixth round, Ali's cornerman Wali Muhammad told Ali, "Champ, he's getting tired."

Ali replied, "I know; I'll get him in a couple of rounds."

By the eighth round, George Foreman was exhausted. His legs were rubbery, and his punches had no force behind them. He threw one wild right and nearly fell out of the ring when it missed. But Ali was tired, too. He knew he would have to end this fight now. And so, with only a few seconds left in the eighth round, he hit Foreman on the jaw with a chopping right. Those who saw the punch connect never forgot it. Foreman seemed to fall in slow motion. First his arms flew out, and then his head fell forward, followed by his huge body. Although he was on his feet by the count of nine, the referee, Zack Clayton, stopped the fight. One look into Foreman's dazed eyes told Clayton that the boxer was thoroughly beaten.

The crowd went wild. "Ali, Ali, Ali!" they screamed, "Ali! Ali! Ali!" They felt as if they had witnessed a miracle. And the whole event *did* seem like an incredible dream. Muhammad Ali had evened the score. He had regained the crown that had been unfairly taken from him.

As a crush of friends, fans, police, and reporters swarmed into the ring, Ali looked a little scared for the first time that night. A few minutes later, a storm broke, drenching the stadium. If it had hit a few minutes earlier, the fight would have been suspended.

Back in his dressing room, Muhammad Ali told reporters to eat their words, just as he had after first defeating Sonny Liston. "I told you this man don't have no punch! I told you this would be a total mismatch!" But this time he sounded playful, not angry. This time, the reporters laughed along with him.

It took George Foreman several years to overcome the bitterness of his defeat. At first he blamed the referee for counting too fast. He also claimed that he had been drugged.

"I should have just said the best man won," he later admitted. "Muhammad Ali gave me a dose of that big right hand. He won fair and square, and now I'm just proud to be part of the Ali legend."

George Foreman continued to fight on and off for several years. Eventually, he came out of retirement to regain the heavyweight championship at age 45. After he gave up boxing, he launched a successful business career.

He has promoted everything from mufflers to his best-selling low-fat grills. He is far from the angry young man he used to be. These days, people really *like* George Foreman.

Muhammad Ali also continued to fight for years after "The Rumble in the Jungle." In fact, he went on fighting long after he should have retired. Repeated blows to the head took a heavy toll on him. They resulted in the condition known as Parkinson's syndrome. Today Muhammad Ali can no longer do the things he used to. He walks slowly. His hands shake. He is unable to move his facial muscles. He has difficulty speaking. But his mind is as quick as ever.

In 1996, Ali was secretly invited to light the flame opening the Summer Olympics in Atlanta. Could he do it? Ali thought so, although some close to him thought he shouldn't even try. They thought his medical condition might make him drop the torch, an embarrassment that three billion viewers would see. But as the lights went up in the Olympic stadium, revealing Muhammad Ali, the crowd roared. Still brimming with confidence, Ali accepted the relay torch from champion swimmer Janet Evans. Although his arm was shaking, he held the torch firmly and lit the flame. As he did so, people around the world wept.

On November 9, 2005, at a White House ceremony, Muhammad Ali received the U.S.

Presidential Medal of Freedom. The same government that had once stripped him of his world championship now recognized him as the genuine American hero he has become.

Michael Jordan:
Saving the Best for Last

In the history of American sports, few athletes have made more of an impact than Michael Jeffrey Jordan. After a brilliant college career at the University of North Carolina, Jordan was drafted by the Chicago Bulls in 1984. In his

NBA rookie season, he led the league in scoring and played brilliant defense—pulling down 534 rebounds and averaging 2.4 steals per game. It seemed that Jordan had no weaknesses as a player. He was as great on defense as he was on offense. Not surprisingly, Bulls ticket sales nearly doubled. On the road, more people came to see Michael Jordan and the Bulls than any other team.

Throughout Jordan's career, observers struggled to find words to describe his incredible talent. Some called him a basketball genius—the Einstein of his sport. Others said that he played basketball better than anyone in the world did anything else.

What made Jordan so great? As one writer wrote, "He could hold the ball better with one hand than most players could with two. And he possessed an unmatchable, explosive first step."

In addition, Jordan possessed incredible jumping ability. People called him "Air Jordan" or "His Airness." He seemed to defy gravity as he soared to the basket. Apparently, he could score whenever he wanted to. He scored 50 points or more in 31 regular season games and 40 or more points in 38 *playoff* games. He won more scoring titles than any other player in NBA history.

Boston Celtics great Larry Bird once said, "On the scale of one to ten, if all the other superstars are eight, [Jordan's] a ten." And after Jordan scored 63 points against a great Celtics team at Boston Garden, Bird said, "That was God disguised as Michael Jordan."

Not only was Michael Jordan the league's most talented player; he was also one of its hardest-working. Unlike other stars who seem to coast on their talent, he was always the first player at practices and the last to leave. His amazing work ethic was matched by the ferocious way he played the game. Even as a small boy, he hated to lose. Baseball, card games, Monopoly—you name it; Michael Jordan would go all out to win.

"I despise losing, and I would do anything to avoid it," Jordan once said. "I never feel I've lost until the game is over."

If Michael Jordan was fearsome on the court, he was a marketing dream off the court. Of course, there had been many black superstars before him. But none had connected with white America the way Michael Jordan did. His handsome face, his smile, the grace with which he conducted himself in public seemed ready-made to sell products. Not surprisingly, Nike sold 2.3 million pairs of Air Jordan sneakers and another $18 million worth of his clothing in Jordan's rookie year alone.

Yet even after Michael Jordan became the most famous athlete on the planet, he never lost his intensity. By 1998, Jordan and the Chicago Bulls had won five World Championships. "He still plays every game like a playoff game," people marveled.

But in 1998, the Bulls were showing their age. Jordan was 35. The Bulls' great small forward, Scottie Pippen, was 33, while rebounding ace Dennis Rodman was 37. What's more, change was in the air in Chicago. It was clear that Phil Jackson, the Bulls' coach, was going to leave the team. Despite guiding the Bulls to five world championships, he and the Bulls' general manager, Jerry Krause, didn't get along. Many thought that Krause was jealous of the respect that the Bulls' players had for Jackson, who had been a fine reserve player for the New York Knicks. In contrast, none of the Bulls respected Krause, who seemed to demand most of the credit for the team's success.

"I don't care if it's 82–0 this year," Krause told Jackson shortly before the 1997–1998 season opened. "You're gone."

Michael Jordan had hinted that if Phil Jackson left the Bulls, he would leave too. After Jackson left and the Bulls hired a new coach, Jordan explained his unwillingness to play for the new coach to a group of kids at a summer basketball camp.

"Let me give you a comparison," he told the campers. "If you grew up your entire life with one set of parents, and you got to a certain age and you were assigned new parents, what would you want? Would you want to stay with your original parents or with the new parents? The old parents were the people who taught you everything, fed you, helped you through certain periods in your life. Now they say you have to go through the same process with new parents? That's how I feel about playing for another coach."

So 1998 was the last year Michael Jordan would be a Chicago Bull. But, like the rest of the Bulls, he wanted one more championship.

Standing in the Bulls' way in the NBA Finals were the Utah Jazz. The Jazz were led by two future Hall of Famers—255-pound power forward Karl "The Mailman" Malone and speedy point guard John Stockton. The Bulls had narrowly beaten the Jazz in last year's Finals. Now many experts predicted that an older and wiser Jazz team would become the new world champs. They pointed out that the Bulls had barely survived an exhausting seven-game series against the Indiana Pacers. In contrast, the Jazz had had a relatively easy time of it against the Los Angeles Lakers. As a result, they were well rested.

"Dead men dribbling," some called the Bulls. They didn't seem to realize that money and fame hadn't weakened Michael Jordan's fighting spirit.

The Finals started in Salt Lake City, a city 4,000 feet above sea level. Perhaps the Bulls had difficulty adjusting to the thin mountain air. Perhaps they were still recovering from the draining series with the Pacers. They looked sluggish. Although they picked up the pace in the fourth quarter, Utah still beat them in overtime, 88–85. Game Two was a different story. In it, the

Bulls played tough defense. They limited John Stockton's movement and therefore his ability to feed Karl Malone the ball. The Bulls also saved much of their offense for the last quarter, when Michael Jordan hit four baskets and shot five of six free throws. In contrast, Karl Malone did not score a basket in the second half. The Bulls won, 93–88.

Back in Chicago, Game Three also went the Bulls' way. Their brilliant defense stole the ball and cut off passing lanes. They seemed to know exactly how to defend against Utah's rather predictable offensive schemes. As a result, Utah seemed to be always off-balance, always forcing their shots. The final score was lopsided in Chicago's favor, 96–54. Utah had scored the fewest points in any NBA game since the introduction of the shot clock.

Another Chicago victory gave the Bulls a 3-games-to-1 advantage. However, in Game Five, Karl Malone reminded the Chicago crowd why he was a superstar. He had a fantastic night, scoring 39 points, while Michael Jordan made only 9 of 26 shots, and Scottie Pippen made only 2 of 16. The Jazz won, 83–81. Afterward, Coach Jackson blamed his team's defeat on too much pre-game hype. Perhaps the Bulls were too eager to taste the victory champagne. Perhaps the Jazz had simply adjusted to the Bulls' style of play. But one thing was clear: If the Bulls were to take the NBA Finals, they would have to win in Salt Lake City.

Phil Jackson told Jordan, "Michael—we'll need one more game. We'll have to win it on the road. I think it's better this way."

It would definitely be more of a challenge. Utah fans were known for their intensity. Sometimes Jackson suspected that a large and vocal home crowd influenced the way the officials called the game. And if the Bulls didn't win Game Six, the Utah players would smell blood as they headed into Game Seven. To make matters even more difficult for the Bulls, Scottie Pippen had badly injured his back in Game Three. Although he had received some cortisone shots, they didn't help much with the pain. With such an injury, he wouldn't even be on the court during a regular-season game.

Pippen started Game Six at Salt Lake's Delta Center, but his back injury severely limited his ability to move. He played seven minutes and then went to the locker room. He didn't return until the third quarter. His teammates Dennis Rodman and Ron Harper were not scorers. Reserve forward Toni Kukoc was unreliable. Steve Kerr was a fine shooter, but with Pippen out, Utah would be able to guard him more closely. If the Bulls were to win the championship, Michael Jordan would once more have to carry the team.

But Jordan was no longer young. He could no longer play 48 minutes of intense offense *and* defense. So he paced himself, saving his energy for the all-important fourth quarter. He did less rebounding than he normally did. Still, by halftime, he had 23 while Karl Malone had only 11. Utah's failure to put the game away while Jordan was conserving his energy gave the Bulls confidence that they would win.

In the second half, Scottie Pippen came back, but he was hobbled by his back injury. As the fourth quarter began, Utah had a narrow 66–61 lead. With five minutes left to play, the score was tied at 77. In the next few minutes, Michael Jordan missed four jump shots in a row. The Bulls' assistant coach, Tex Winter, told Phil Jackson, "Look, he can't get any elevation on his shot. His legs are gone."

During a time-out two minutes later, Jackson told Jordan to forget about making jump shots. "Just take it to the basket," he said.

Jordan agreed. "They haven't got a center in now, so the way is clear."

Although Karl Malone hit a twenty-foot jumper to put the Jazz ahead 83–79, Jordan drove to the basket and drew a foul. With 2:07 left on the clock, he hit both foul shots, cutting Utah's lead to two points. When Jordan again drove to the basket, John Stockton once again fouled him. Again Jordan hit both free throws to tie the score at 83–83 with 59.2 seconds left. During the Bulls' next timeout, Coach Jackson and Jordan talked about what kind of shot he would take in the remaining seconds of the game.

When Jackson reminded him that his legs were tired, Jordan replied, "I've got my second wind now."

"If you have to go for the jumper," Jackson advised him, "you've got to follow through better. You haven't been following through."

As play resumed, Utah brought the ball upcourt slowly and deliberately. When Chicago double-teamed Malone, he passed across the court to Stockton, who hit a beautiful 24-foot jumper. This three-pointer made the score 86–83 in favor of the Jazz. The crowd at Delta Center breathed more easily.

But when the Bulls got the ball, Jordan drove down the right side and laid the ball up for a basket. With Utah leading 86–85, Stockton came across the halfcourt line, let the clock wind down a little, and then worked the ball to Malone. But even before Malone got the ball, Jordan sneaked in behind him. Then, with his body at exactly the right angle to avoid fouling Malone, he reached out and swiped the ball away.

"Karl never saw me coming," Jordan later said.

From then on in, he knew exactly what to do. There would be no timeout. He would keep the ball.

"I would have taken that shot with five people on me," he told reporters at the post-game press conference. "I had no intention of passing the ball under any circumstances. I figured I stole the ball, and it was my opportunity to win or lose the game."

And so, after letting the clock run down another seven seconds, Jordan started his drive past Jazz defender Bryon Russell. Utah didn't dare double-team Jordan, because doing so would free up Kerr, a dangerous outside shooter. When Jordan faked to his right, Russell reached. Then Jordan pulled up sharply. Russell sprawled to his left, nearly falling, as Jordan squared up and shot. This time, his form was perfect. As the Utah crowd looked on in dismay, the ball swished into the basket. Chicago had the lead with 6.6 seconds left to play.

John Stockton missed a hurried jumper, and then the buzzer sounded. The Bulls had won, 87–86. For the sixth time, Michael Jordan had led his team to a world championship. He had scored the Bulls' last eight points, and 45 in all.

"I love it when it comes down to that one moment and it's all in my hands," he explained. "No matter what the game is or who you're playing against, you have to want the ball. The clock, the pressure—you block all that out. All you think about is what you have to do to win."

Michael Jordan had played dozens of outstanding games throughout his career. But Game Six of the 1998 NBA Finals stands as his masterpiece.

The First Family of Football:
Archie, Peyton, and Eli Manning

As quarterback for the New Orleans Saints throughout the 1970s, Archie Manning tasted defeat far more often than victory. Manning had been a star quarterback who had led the University of Mississippi (Ole Miss) Rebels to three winning seasons. As a result, he had been the second player taken in the 1969 NFL draft. Manning continued to play well for the Saints, but most years the team around him was terrible. During one Saints loss, even Archie's own little boys, Cooper and Peyton, joined in booing the team as they sat in the stands with their mother. Not knowing any better, they were simply copying the fans around them.

"If Archie Manning had played for Dallas, he'd be in the Hall of Fame now," said Cowboys Hall of Fame quarterback Roger Staubach. Because Archie's pro football career had been so frustrating, some expected him to push his sons into the sport. In this way, they thought, he could fulfill his dreams of glory through them. But Archie didn't, for one good reason. He had been around plenty of ex-football players who tried to pressure their sons into becoming pro football players. Usually, the results weren't pretty.

"Ninety-nine times out of a hundred, it doesn't happen," said Archie. As he had seen, boys who are pressured to make the pros—and don't get there—often become angry with their fathers. As a result, the father-son relationship suffers.

For Archie Manning, faith and family always came before football. He cherished his relationships with his sons, especially since he had never felt very close to his own father. When Archie was fifteen, his father had a stroke. A few years later, he took his own life. Now as a father, Archie made sure to find time for his boys. Since he and his wife, Olivia, had bought a house in New Orleans, he often brought them to Saints practices. There they threw around a toy football as their dad and his teammates practiced with a real one. But it wasn't all football for the Mannings. Archie and Olivia didn't let their boys play tackle football until they were twelve years old. They also tried to get them interested in activities besides football, such as fishing and playing the piano.

"It wasn't football I was pushing, it was involvement," Archie later wrote. Still, the boys preferred football from the beginning. By the time they reached their teens, oldest brother Cooper was a talented receiver, and Peyton was a natural quarterback. It was too early to tell about Eli, who was five years younger than Peyton.

Archie and Olivia enrolled the boys at Isidore Newman, a private school in New Orleans. Although Newman wasn't known for football, both Cooper and Peyton stood out as members of the Newman "Greenies." Peyton was the starting quarterback, and Cooper was his star wide receiver. When Cooper enrolled at Ole Miss, Peyton expected to follow him. But then doctors discovered that Cooper had a serious spinal condition. This condition forced him to quit athletics. As a result, Peyton began to think about other schools besides Ole Miss. After considering offers from over sixty schools, he decided to attend the University of Tennessee. For decades, the Tennessee Volunteers had been a powerhouse in the Southeast Conference.

After joining the Volunteers, Peyton quickly became known as "Caveman" because he spent so much time in dark rooms studying football film.

"I was determined to the point of being obsessed," admits Peyton. His hard work soon paid off. When the two quarterbacks in front of him were injured, he beat out another freshman for the starting job. Under Peyton's leadership, the Volunteers had four winning seasons. In Peyton's senior year, he led the Vols to an 11–1 record. The team narrowly missed the national championship when it lost to Nebraska in the Orange Bowl. Peyton's statistics, though, were second to none. He set a record for career passing yardage in the SEC with 11,201 yards. Because of what he had achieved at Tennessee and his maturity on and off the field, the Indianapolis Colts selected him first in the 1998 NFL draft. In signing with the Colts, he would be paid $48 million for six years. This was 96 times what his dad had signed for.

"What do you plan to do with all that money?" someone asked Peyton after he signed with the Colts.

"Earn it," he replied.

In a way, Peyton Manning faced a situation with the Colts very much like the one his dad had faced with the Saints. Indianapolis had gone 3–13 in 1997, and there was no guarantee that the Colts would ever become a winning team. Still, Peyton respected the Colts' new owner, Robert Irsay. In addition, his dad Archie knew and respected the Colts head coach Jim Mora. And Peyton had great confidence in himself.

"You know, Mr. Irsay, I'll win for you," he had told the Colts' owner shortly before the draft.

But just as Rome wasn't built in a day, Peyton didn't lead the Colts to a winning season in his rookie year. Steve Young, the 49ers' Hall of Fame quarterback, explained how different the NFL was from college football. He said, "The jump from college to the pros is like going from a tricycle to a car on the highway."

The first pass Peyton Manning threw in a Colts preseason game went for a touchdown.

"The season went downhill from there," Peyton later joked, as the Colts quickly lost their first four regular-season games. They finished the season with another 3–13 record. Yet Peyton had done well. True, he threw 28 interceptions, but he also threw for 28 touchdowns. This was a record for a rookie.

"I always had the theory that a quarterback doesn't have a clue until his fifth year," said Hall of Fame coach and broadcaster John Madden.

"But with [Peyton Manning] that goes right out the window."

Still, Peyton's goal was to win, not set records. He would try even harder next year.

The Colts improved greatly in 1999, going 13–3. This was the biggest turnaround in NFL history. Peyton became a master at reading defenses and calling plays at the line of scrimmage. His favorite receiver was the lightning-fast Marvin Harrison. Still, in 2000, the Colts' record slipped to 10–6. In 2001, they were even worse at 6–10. The problem wasn't Peyton. It was the Colts' leaky defense, which had given up more points than any NFL team since 1981. To solve this problem, the Colts fired Jim Mora and hired Tony Dungy, who was known as a defensive mastermind. Like Peyton, Dungy was an intense student of the game. People joked that he watched game film until his eyeballs fell out.

Although the Colts got off to a slow 4–4 start in 2002, they picked up steam and finished 10–6. But in the first round of the playoffs, they fell to the New York Jets in an embarrassing 41–0 loss. Manning had one of the worst games of his career, completing only 14 of 31 passes for 137 yards. Since this was the third playoff game that a Manning-led Colts team had lost, some began to wonder if Peyton had the "right stuff" to win a championship.

The Colts got off to a fast start in 2003, winning their first five games and going on to post a 12–4 record. This time, they beat the Denver Broncos and the Kansas City Chiefs in the playoffs. Then they headed to New England to play the Patriots and Tom Brady. Going into the game, Brady and the Patriots had already beaten Manning and the Colts four straight times. In this game Tom Brady was once again terrific, while Peyton was not. He threw four interceptions in the Colts' 24–14 loss.

In 2004, it seemed the Patriots once again had the Colts' number. In the AFC Championship game, Brady and the Patriots defeated Manning and the Colts 20–3.

After the 2005 season, the Colts once again lost in the playoffs, this time to the Pittsburgh Steelers. Again critics said that Peyton "couldn't win the big one to get to the big one." Others agreed that his passing totals were great, but that he "choked" in big games.

As the 2006 season wore on, the Colts again ran up an impressive record, finishing the season at 12–4. Once again Peyton Manning was like a machine at quarterback. He finished the regular season with a 65 percent completion rate and 4,397 yards.

As expected, the Colts won in the first two rounds of the playoffs. The greater test came when they again faced the New England Patriots in the AFC Championship game. Although the Colts had beaten Brady and the Patriots earlier in the season, Brady had a history of excelling in pressure situations. Before 57,000 fans in Indianapolis, the Patriots quickly got off to a 21–3 lead. The Patriots' defenders were batting away many of Manning's passes, making the Colts' offense sputter and stall. It looked as though the New Englanders would once again dash the Colts' Super Bowl hopes. It also looked as if Tom Brady would once again prove to be a better "clutch" quarterback than Peyton Manning. Yet in the locker room at halftime, Tony Dungy looked Peyton in the eye and said, "I'm telling you, this is our game."

Dungy wasn't just saying this to make his quarterback feel better. He truly believed that the Patriots couldn't keep defending against Manning's long bombs. And what happened next proved he was right. In the third quarter, Peyton Manning coolly led his team on two long touchdown drives, tying the game at 21–21. But then New England scored another touchdown. The Colts answered that by scoring a touchdown on a recovered fumble. Three field goals later, New England was up 34–31. When the Colts took the field, there was just 2:17 left to play. This turned out to be plenty of time for Peyton Manning. Like a surgeon, he picked apart the Patriots' defense, taking his team 80 yards down the field for another touchdown.

There was still 1:02 left in the game— enough time for Tom Brady to lead his team to victory. But Tom wasn't so terrific today. With 24 seconds left to play, he threw an interception. As blue and white confetti streamed onto the field, the Colts were on their way to the Super Bowl.

In Super Bowl XLI, the Colts faced the Chicago Bears. The Bears were an excellent defensive team who boasted an NFC-best 13–3 record. The jury was still out, though, on their quarterback, Rex Grossman. He had gotten the team off to a great start, but had slumped badly toward the end of the season. Many Chicago fans hoped that Coach Lovie Smith would bench him in favor of veteran Brian Griese. However, Smith stuck with Grossman.

As the rain came down at Dolphins Stadium in Miami, Bears rookie Devin Hester stunned the crowd by running the opening kickoff back for a 92-yard touchdown. When Peyton Manning threw a deep pass that defensive back Chris Harris intercepted, Colts fans became uneasy. But the Bears couldn't move the ball and were forced to punt. On the Colts' next possession, Peyton spied Reggie Wayne streaking across the field and threw a 53-yard bomb to him for a touchdown. After several turnovers, Rex Grossman threw a short touchdown pass to receiver Muhsin Muhammad. The score now stood at 14–6, since the Colts had failed on their extra-point try. But heading into the second quarter, the Colts scored on an Adam Vinatieri field goal. A few minutes later, Peyton Manning started out a drive with four completions. Then he began handing off to

Dominic Rhodes, who took the ball to the end zone with three straight carries. The Colts led 16–14 at the half.

In the second half, two more Colts field goals made the score 22–14. Growing desperate, Rex Grossman threw a long pass to Muhammad. But Colts defensive back Kelvin Hayden intercepted the pass and returned it 56 yards for a touchdown. When Grossman threw another interception, the Colts knew they had the game in the bag. They called eight straight runs before turning the ball over on downs. Five plays later, the Colts were Super Bowl Champions. MVP Peyton Manning had finally silenced his critics by winning the Big One.

While Peyton Manning was leading the Colts to victory in Super Bowl XLI, father Archie and younger brother Eli were in the stands cheering him on. Eli, who had just completed his second year as quarterback of the New York Giants, told reporters that his brother's victory "definitely sparked something within me. It definitely made me want it even more."

This was something Giants fans were happy to hear, since Eli had *not* had a very good year with the Giants. When he was signed in 2004, the New York fans had expected him to be "just like" his older brother Peyton. When it seemed to be taking Eli longer to mature as an NFL quarterback, they had grown impatient. What they didn't realize was that Eli had never been "just like" Peyton.

Five years younger than outgoing, intense Peyton, Eli had always been the quiet, shy, easygoing Manning. Although his nickname was "Easy," school did not come easily to him. In fact, as a small boy, he struggled to learn to read. But with extra help, he became a fine student. As a teen, he got used to being in Peyton's shadow. Fortunately for Eli, he had inherited the Manning talent for football. A star at Ole Miss, he had been drafted number one by the San Diego Chargers. But when he made it clear that he didn't want to play for the lowly Chargers, they traded him to the New York Giants for quarterback Philip Rivers and two other draft picks.

If big things had been expected of Peyton, enormous things were expected of Eli, and right away. One reason expectations were so high was that big brother Peyton was already a superstar. Another reason was that Eli was playing in the New York area. Unlike the laid-back Midwesterners of Indianapolis, New Yorkers were not known for their patience. When Eli did poorly, angry calls flooded talk radio shows. The media criticized him harshly. And although Eli's first three years with the Giants weren't disastrous, he had clearly failed to live up to what was expected of him.

"This kid's a bust," some reporters wrote.

"Eli's progress right now is not where we want him to be," admitted Giants general manager Jerry Reese. "We want him to be a Pro Bowl guy that can lead us to the Super Bowl."

Given all this pressure, could Eli improve his game? The 2007 season got off to a slow start. In a season-opening loss to Dallas, Eli was slammed to the turf, badly bruising his right shoulder. This injury bothered him for several weeks. Fortunately, the Giants had a strong defense and running game. Five weeks into the season, they were 3–2. After a loss to Dallas and a win against Detroit, the Giants played the Minnesota Vikings. In this game, Eli threw four interceptions as the Giants lost, 41–17.

"Eli the Terrible," screamed the *New York Daily News.* Worse yet, the story spread that Eli was afraid to get hit, that he was "gun shy." According to a poll of NFL players, Eli Manning came in second behind the Bears' Rex Grossman as "easiest quarterback to intimidate."

But just when Giants fans were about to give up on Eli, he guided his team to a thrilling come-from-behind win over the Bears in Chicago. Yet the Giants' roller-coaster ride continued. After a narrow win against the Philadelphia Eagles, they lost to the Washington Redskins at home, 22–10. In this game, both Eli and his receivers played poorly. Either they dropped the ball or Eli missed his targets. Finally, in the sleet and fierce winds of Buffalo, the Giants clinched a playoff spot by defeating the Bills, 38–21. Their next game would be meaningless in terms of making the playoffs. However, since it was against the undefeated New England Patriots, the Giants were determined to play hard. Although they narrowly lost 38–35, they proved that they were no pushovers.

In the first round of the playoffs, Eli and the Giants dominated Tampa Bay, 24–14. After that, they defeated the NFC's top-seeded Dallas Cowboys, 21–17. In the NFC Championship game, they whipped Brett Favre and the Packers 23–20 in sub-zero weather at Green Bay. During this stretch, "Eli the Terrible" completed an outstanding 64.1 percent of his passes, with 8 touchdowns and only 1 interception.

As the Giants headed to the Super Bowl in Glendale, Arizona, they were heavy underdogs. Some were calling the 18–0 Patriots the best team in pro football history. Others named them "the Perfect Patriots." They were expected to join the 1972 Miami Dolphins as the only team in NFL history to be undefeated. But the Giants weren't bothered by all the Patriots' hype.

"We know how good they are. But we know what it takes to beat them," said Eli.

During Super Bowl XLII, the Giants' pass rush battered Tom Brady for most of the game. But with 7:54 left to play, Brady once again did what he was famous for and led the Patriots on an eighty-yard touchdown drive. This made the score 14–10 Patriots with 2:42 left to play.

Thinking the game was as good as over, some members of the media began handing in their MVP ballots. Most had voted for the Patriots' receiver, Wes Welker, who had made 11 catches for 103 yards.

Still, Eli Manning refused to give up.

"Let's go win this thing. Who's with me?" he asked his teammates in the huddle. His words may have sounded corny, but there was quiet confidence in his eyes.

The Giants' miracle drive started with an 11-yard completion. Less than a minute later, running back Brandon Jacobs blasted through for a crucial first down. Two plays later, the Patriots nearly picked off an Eli pass on a broken play. The Giants were still 56 yards from the end zone with 1:15 left.

What followed may be the greatest play in Super Bowl history. On third down and 5, Eli took the snap and looked to his receivers. Almost immediately, three Patriots broke through the Giants' offensive line. Two clawed at Eli's shirt. Another grabbed Eli's shoulder pads and tried to leap on his back.

"Gonna be sacked!" shouted an announcer.

But Eli was the calm eye of the storm. He somehow kept his feet and scrambled back a few yards. As the Patriot defenders swarmed after him, he squared his shoulders and threw a 32-yard pass to David Tyree, a special-teams player who had caught only seven passes all season. Tyree leaped and caught the ball. Then, as Patriots safety Rodney Harrison did his best to pry the ball loose, Tyree pinned it against his helmet like a medal, came down with it, and kept it from touching the ground.

"Some things just don't make sense," David Tyree later said. "I guess you could put that catch up there with those."

Four plays later, Plaxico Burress caught Eli's fade pass in the end zone to make the score 17–14. When Tom Brady failed to connect with his receivers with 35 seconds left to play, the Giants were Super Bowl Champions. Now it was Archie and Peyton Manning's turn to watch proudly as Eli received the Super Bowl MVP trophy.

Giants defensive end Michael Strahan probably summed it up best. "[Eli's] not Peyton Manning's little brother anymore," Strahan said. "He's not Eli who slumps. None of that. Eli Manning is the world champion."

Victory hadn't come easy for Eli "Easy" Manning. But it couldn't be sweeter.

After his sons Peyton and Eli had become stars in the NFL, people often asked Archie Manning when it was he had first realized that his boys had great football talent. His response was surprising.

"I wasn't looking for it. I refused to judge their play that way," he said. To him, the sensible approach was to let the boys enjoy what they were doing. The rest would take care of itself.

"The bottom line is that if they'd chosen basketball or golf or tennis . . . or if they'd quit sport entirely and elected to play the piano, I'd have said 'Godspeed.' As long as it helped round out their lives."

Such a "no-pressure" approach surely enabled Peyton and Eli to develop at their own pace and to experience playing football as a joy, rather than an ordeal. Archie Manning may never have won a Super Bowl or made the Hall of Fame. But judging from the lives of his sons, he is certainly an "All-Pro" father.

Broken Records:
Baseball and Steroids

Ever since baseball was first played in the mid-1800s, it has been a beloved national pastime. But in the mid-1990s, America's love of the game was put to the test. In August 1994, major league players went on strike when owners tried to limit the amount of money they could earn in one season. Because of the strike-shortened season, there was no World Series—for the first time since 1905. Even though the owners gave in, and the strike ended by opening day of 1995, baseball fans were still disgusted.

"Why should millionaire ballplayers go on strike against billionaire owners?" they wondered. As a result, many of them turned their back on the sport. Attendance suffered.

In 1998, though, the fans started coming back. The reason was the home-run race between St. Louis Cardinals first baseman Mark McGwire and Chicago Cubs right fielder Sammy Sosa. When the season began, both stars got off to a fast start. By the end of May, McGwire had slugged 27 home runs. If he kept up this blistering pace, he would easily break Roger Maris's single-season home run record of 61, which had stood for 37 years. Meanwhile, "Slammin' Sammy" Sosa of the Cubs was hitting home runs nearly as quickly as McGwire. As the season wore on, huge crowds turned out to watch both men try to break Maris's record. It seemed that this home-run derby was just the "shot in the arm" that baseball needed.

Even better yet for baseball, both players were fan favorites. McGwire was a gentle giant who hugged his son, a St. Louis batboy, after each home run he hit. Sosa was a cheerful Dominican who blew a kiss skyward, to honor his deceased mother, after every home run *he* hit. Both men took time to sign autographs. Both gave lots of money to charity. When McGwire or

Sosa took batting practice, crowds of reporters and fans gathered to watch balls sail over the outfield fences.

By the end of the season, both men had easily broken Maris's record. McGwire won the home-run crown by hitting 70 home runs. Sosa came in second, hitting 66. Both appeared on the cover of *Sports Illustrated*. Both were named Sportsman of the Year. Sosa won the National League Most Valuable Player Award. Together the two sluggers were credited with bringing new life, and profits, to baseball.

But in the midst of all the celebration, one man questioned McGwire's and Sosa's achievements. During the summer, a reporter named Steve Wilstein had noticed a bottle of pills in Mark McGwire's locker. The bottle was labeled androstenedione, or "andro" for short. Andro was a chemical that artificially boosted testosterone, the male sex hormone. In other words, it was a steroid that helped build muscle. With added muscle came added power. With added power came—more home runs?

When Wilstein wrote a story on McGwire's use of andro, baseball officials quickly pointed out that the chemical was perfectly legal. This was true. However, officials failed to mention that the Olympics and the NFL had already banned it. Rather than join him in questioning McGwire's use of andro, other reporters accused Wilstein of trying to destroy baseball.

Another person who questioned McGwire's and Sosa's success was San Francisco Giants left fielder Barry Bonds. A proud man, Bonds considered himself the best player in baseball. He was probably right. He had won the Most Valuable Player award three times. Not only could he hit for power, but he also hit for average, stole bases, and was a Golden Glove outfielder. In 1998, Bonds became the first player to both hit 400 home runs and steal 400 bases. Yet no one paid much attention to him because of the home-run race between McGwire and Sosa. This lack of recognition angered Bonds. He knew he was more talented than both McGwire and Sosa. To him, they were players who could hit the long ball but do little else.

What's more, Bonds suspected the two men were "juicing"—using steroids. Anyone could see it from the change in their bodies. McGwire had always been a big man, but now he was musclebound. And Sammy Sosa, who had once been a skinny shortstop, was equally buff. In fact, the two looked more like weightlifters than like ballplayers. Seeing all the attention the two "home run heroes" were getting, Bonds decided he would follow their lead. In 1999, he too came to spring training with a "new, improved" body. He had gained fifteen pounds of muscle in one hundred days.

"You look like the Incredible Hulk," other players told him. They wondered what on earth he had been doing in the off-season.

Bonds explained that his newfound muscle was due to lifting weights and taking dietary supplements. He had a new weight trainer named Greg Anderson. Anderson had been a childhood friend of Bonds when they both lived near San Francisco. Now Anderson had connections with a dietary supplement company called BALCO (Bay Area Laboratory Co-operative). With the aid of Anderson and BALCO, Bonds began hitting home runs faster than he ever had before. But he had put on too much muscle too fast and blew out an elbow. (Joint problems are one side effect of steroid use.) In 1999, Bonds played in only 102 games.

In 2000, the thirty-six-year-old Bonds had his best season so far—batting .306 and hitting 49 home runs, even though he missed nearly 20 games with another injury. Baseball fans viewed Bonds's numbers as impressive but odd. Most baseball players' skills go downhill after age 35. Yet it seemed Bonds was just warming up. In 2001, he had the greatest offensive season in the history of baseball, setting a new home-run record with 73—averaging one home run every seven at-bats. This was even better than Babe Ruth's best rate. It was also three times better than the rate at which Bonds had hit home runs when he was ten years younger.

Despite Barry Bonds's incredible achievements, fans outside of San Francisco were uneasy about him. For one thing, he didn't look at all like his rookie photos. When Bonds broke into the majors, he was long and lean, like a greyhound. Now he looked more like a cartoon action figure than a baseball player. Even his head looked bigger. People also felt it was strange that he was breaking the home run record so soon after it had been set. After all, Roger Maris's old record had stood for nearly forty years.

"The balls I used to line off the walls are lining out [of the ballpark]," said Bonds. "I can't tell you why."

Soon rumors began spreading that Bonds was on steroids. Suspicions grew when federal agents raided BALCO. There they discovered documents with baseball stars' names on them, including those of Jason Giambi, Gary Sheffield, and Barry Bonds. Many of the documents were records of the drugs and dosages that different players were taking. The records showed that Bonds had been taking two different steroids known as "The Clear" and "The Cream." Both were undetectable by standard drug testing.

On December 4, 2003, Barry Bonds testified under oath before a grand jury investigating BALCO. Several athletes had already testified. Before they did, the government informed them that they would not be prosecuted if they told the truth. However, if any of them lied under oath, the government would charge them with perjury.

Even though Bonds had also been told that he would not be prosecuted if he told the truth, he insisted that he had taken "The Clear" thinking it was flaxseed oil. This is a harmless product sold at health-food stores.

"When [Greg Anderson] said it was flaxseed oil, I just said, 'Whatever,'" Bonds claimed. He also told the grand jury that he had rubbed "The Cream" on his body, thinking it was arthritis medicine.

People who knew Bonds found this hard to believe. He had long had a reputation for being fanatical about his health routine. He would never use something unless he knew exactly what it was. Also, Yankees first baseman Jason Giambi had already told the grand jury that Bonds had introduced him to Greg Anderson. Giambi said he had paid Bonds's trainer more than $10,000 for steroids.

Although the BALCO investigation was supposed to be secret, reporters soon broke the story that it involved steroid use by some of the biggest stars in sports, including Giambi and Bonds.

"Lyin' King!" New York newspapers called Giambi.

"Bonds's home run record has been exposed as a steroid lie," wrote sports columnist Thomas Boswell.

Hall of Fame slugger Reggie Jackson was equally harsh. "Henry Aaron never hit 50 home runs in a season, so you're going to tell me that you're a greater hitter than Henry Aaron? I mean, come on, now. There is no way you outperform Aaron and Ruth and Mays at that level."

And there was still more bad news for Barry Bonds. In March 2005, his former girlfriend Kim Bell testified before the BALCO grand jury. During her testimony, she described the acne on Bonds's back, his shrunken testicles, and his outbursts of rage. When asked if Bonds's head had grown larger, she said she thought she could see the plates in his skull. All these were known side effects of steroid use.

When reporters questioned Bonds about steroids, he complained that they had it in for him.

"My family is tired," he said. "I'm tired. You guys wanted to hurt me bad enough. You finally got there . . . So now go pick on a different person. I'm done."

But as retired slugger Jose Canseco reminded America, Bonds wasn't the only one in hot water because of steroids. In his 2005 tell-all book, *Juiced*, Canseco wrote that he and Mark McGwire had injected steroids while they were teammates on the Oakland Athletics. Furthermore, Canseco claimed that 85% of major league ballplayers took steroids. By now, baseball had imposed penalties for players who failed drug tests. In a 2003 random drug test, 5 to 7 percent of major leaguers tested positive for steroid use.

In 2005, the uproar over steroids grew louder. In May, Congress ordered baseball stars Jose Canseco, Mark McGwire, Sammy Sosa, Rafael Palmeiro, and Curt Schilling to testify before a special panel. Barry Bonds didn't testify before the panel because he was already being investigated for perjury as a result of his BALCO testimony.

As the ballplayers sat in front of members of Congress, they no longer looked like heroes. In fact, Mark McGwire looked as if he was ready to cry. Each time he was asked whether he had taken performance-enhancing drugs, he replied, "I'm not here to talk about the past." Those watching him chuckled and shook their heads.

Sammy Sosa was no more truthful. He claimed to need a translator, even though he spoke perfectly good English. Then he stated that he had never used illegal performance-enhancing drugs. A few years later, reporters would find out that he had tested positive for steroid use during the random drug tests conducted in 2003.

Baltimore Orioles slugger Rafael Palmeiro pointed to the members of Congress. "Let me start by telling you this," he said. "I have never taken steroids. Period." A few months later, he tested positive for steroid use and was suspended for ten games.

The San Francisco Giants wished the whole steroid issue would go away. Barry Bonds was their big draw. Without him, the team was not a contender. They wanted to see Bonds break the career home run record of 755 set by Henry Aaron. After several more great years, Bonds finally did break the record in 2007, when he was 43 years old. But by this time, most fans outside of San Francisco were convinced Bonds had taken steroids. In cities around America, they jeered him and held up insulting signs. At the end of the season, the Giants did not offer to renew his contract. No other major league team wanted to sign him. In November, 2007, he was indicted on four counts of perjury in connection with the government's BALCO investigation. Bonds would never play major league baseball again. In April, 2011, he was convicted on one count of obstruction of justice. (The jury could not agree on the other three counts.) In December, 2011, Bonds was sentenced to a month of home confinement and two years of probation. He plans to appeal the conviction.

In 2007, pitching great Roger "the Rocket" Clemens also became linked with steroid use. After he denied using steroids under oath before Congress, the Justice Department began to investigate him. He was indicted for perjury on August 19, 2010. Clemens's first trial, in July 2011, ended after two days when prosecutors mistakenly introduced banned evidence, resulting in a mistrial. A second trial is scheduled for April 2012.

In 2009, reporters broke the story that New York Yankees superstar Alex Rodriguez had also tested positive for steroid use in 2003. Unlike Bonds and Clemens, Rodriguez admitted he used steroids from 2001 to 2003. Since players could not be suspended for steroid use during these years, Rodriguez was not disciplined.

In spring 2010, Mark McGwire finally admitted using steroids. He is now the hitting coach for the St. Louis Cardinals.

Barry Bonds still claims he did nothing wrong. However, in spring training in 2005, he came as close as he ever has to admitting using steroids. Speaking with two reporters, he said, "All this stuff about supplements, protein shakes, whatever . . . If I can't go out there [to play], and somebody pays $60 for a ticket, and I'm not in the lineup, who's getting cheated? Not me.

"There are far worse things like cocaine, heroin, and those types of things.

"So we all make mistakes. We all do things. We need to turn the page. We need to forget about the past and let us play the game. We're entertainers. Let us entertain."

But *is* baseball simply entertainment? If so, does that mean it's perfectly okay to use steroids to break records set by players who *didn't* use steroids? And what about players who do not want to use steroids because of the serious health risks connected with them? These risks include heart attack, stroke, testicular cancer, liver damage, joint problems, abscesses, and extreme mood swings. If some players use steroids and get away with it, doesn't that mean every player has to use steroids to stay competitive? If so, what message does this send young people? Several high-school athletes have already died as a result of steroid use.

These questions don't have easy answers. One thing that's certain, though, is that since baseball put a strict drug-testing policy in place in 2005, no player has come close to hitting sixty home runs in a season. Yet outlaw chemists are still trying to come up with new, undetectable steroids. And law enforcement is still trying to come up with better drug tests.

Very soon, stars from baseball's "steroid era" will be eligible for the Hall of Fame. Some argue that these stars should be elected to the Hall despite taking performance-enhancing drugs. They say that these players were simply giving the public what it wanted to see: lots of home runs. Others argue that players who took steroids should not be admitted, that their records are forever tainted. They say that electing players such as Bonds, McGwire, Sosa, and Clemens to the Hall of Fame wouldn't be fair to stars like Hank Aaron, who achieved great things without taking performance-enhancing drugs. Still others say that players who took steroids should be elected to the Hall of Fame, but that an asterisk (*) would indicate that their records were set with the help of drugs.

The steroid debate continues. No one knows when, or if, it will end.

The Perfect Game That Wasn't

In a perfect game, a pitcher faces the minimum number of batters—27 for a nine-inning game. He allows no hits and no walks, and the fielders behind him commit no errors. Major league baseball has existed for over 130 years. In that time, pitchers have thrown only 20 perfect games. Many of baseball's greatest—men like Steve Carlton, Nolan Ryan, and Greg Maddox— have never pitched one. So it's no wonder that pitching a "perfecto" is considered the rarest feat in baseball, if not in all of sports.

It's a safe bet that none of the 17,000 fans that filed into Detroit's Comerica Park on the afternoon of June 2, 2010 suspected that he or she was about to see baseball history. In fact, what the fans would soon witness was something even rarer than a perfect game. They would see a perfect game that wasn't.

Detroit pitcher Armando Galarraga was an unlikely figure to play a part in baseball history. The tall, slender right-hander was not a star—in fact, the 28-year-old Venezuelan had bounced back and forth between the major and minor leagues. In 2008, his rookie year, he won 13 games while losing only 7. As a result, he had finished fifth in voting for the American League Rookie of the Year. But in 2009, Galarraga did poorly, winning only 6 games while losing 10. His earned run average was a dismal 5.64. During 2010 spring training, he had failed to impress the Tigers' management and had been sent down to their triple-A minor league club. Then in May he was brought back up and put into the starting rotation. His ERA was a mediocre 4.50 as of June 1. But like most major league teams, the Tigers needed all the pitching they could get. They were locked in a race for the division lead with the Minnesota Twins and Chicago White Sox. They knew Galarraga had talent. Now if he could only become more consistent . . .

On this mild Wednesday afternoon, it seemed that Galarraga had his best stuff. His slider was breaking on both sides of the plate. His 93-mile-per-hour fastball had outstanding life, rising on some hitters and tailing off on others. It moved around the plate like a firefly, making it difficult for hitters to follow. The first Cleveland batter, Trevor Crowe, hit a sky-high fly ball that speedy Detroit centerfielder Austin Jackson easily caught. The second batter, Shin-Soo Choo, grounded out to first; and the third batter, Austin Kearns, lined out to first. In the second inning, all three Cleveland batters grounded out. The next few innings were much like the first two. Some Cleveland batters would hit the ball hard, but right at a Detroit fielder. Others would meekly ground out to an infielder. Meanwhile, the Detroit Tigers' power-hitting first baseman, Miguel Cabrera, had launched a ball into the seats in left field, putting the Tigers up by a score of 1–0.

By the bottom of the fifth inning, Tigers fans were becoming energized. They knew that Armando Galarraga was pitching a perfect game, and they desperately wanted him to succeed. Galarraga quickly disposed of Travis Hafner, who hit a fly ball that left fielder Johnny Damon caught in foul territory. Then Jhonny Peralta grounded out to Galarraga. After that, Russell Branyan hit a ball that bounced off the mound right over to third baseman Brandon Inge, who easily threw Branyan out. So far Galarraga was cruising, pounding the strike zone with his slider and fastball. The location of his pitches, coupled with their velocity, kept the Cleveland hitters off balance, making it difficult for them to get good wood on the ball.

In the sixth inning, the first Indians batter, Mark Grudzielanek, struck out swinging on a ball out of the strike zone. The second batter, Mike Redmond, flied out to centerfielder Austin Jackson, and Jason Donald lined out to center. It had taken Armando Galarraga only eight pitches to dispose of the three Cleveland batters.

By now, the Detroit fans were beginning to suspect that they might be watching a very special ballgame. If Galarraga were to pitch a perfect game, it would be the first one in Tigers history. The Tigers' faithful could tell their grandchildren they were there.

The seventh and eighth were one-two-three innings for Galarraga. He was working swiftly, efficiently. In the top of the eighth, the fans were on their feet cheering as Galarraga got Russell Branyan to ground out to second. Only three more outs to go!

Detroit then scored two runs in the bottom of the eighth inning to take a 3–0 lead.

In the top of the ninth, Detroit fans groaned as the Indians' first batter, Mark Grudzielanek, hit a long fly ball to the deepest part of left centerfield. It looked like it would surely fall for an extra-base hit. But rookie centerfielder Austin Jackson was amazingly fast. After a long run across the outfield grass, he sprinted over to the warning track, twisted, and caught the ball over his left shoulder.

"Austin Jackson in left center field! A sparkling play!" cried the Detroit broadcasters.

Armando Galarraga grinned as he watched Jackson catch the ball. The stadium exploded in cheers. Jackson's miracle catch had saved Galarraga's perfect game.

After Indians catcher Mike Redmond grounded out to shortstop, one more batter stood between the tall young pitcher and baseball immortality. That was Indians rookie shortstop Jason Donald.

Armando Galarraga's first pitch to Jason Donald was a strike. His second was a ball. Donald hit the third pitch for a foul ball strike. Now ahead of the batter, Galarraga threw a pitch on the outside part of the plate that Donald hit weakly to the right of first baseman Miguel Cabrera. As Cabrera ranged to his right to field the ball, Galarraga raced over to cover first base. He got there ahead of Donald. Cabrera's throw landed in Galarraga's glove as the pitcher reached out his long leg and touched first base. It was a play that major leaguers practice over and over in spring training. Timing and teamwork are what make it work. This time, it appeared that Cabrera and Galarraga had executed the play perfectly. Galarraga began to raise his arms in triumph when he looked at first base umpire Jim Joyce. But rather than signaling that Donald was out, Joyce did something shocking. He threw his arms out horizontally, indicating that the Cleveland hitter had beaten the throw.

Armando Galarraga immediately put his arms down. He smiled a wry smile. It was the kind of smile a person gives when they suspect that someone is playing a joke on them. "Are you kidding?" his look seemed to say.

Detroit first baseman Miguel Cabrera's reaction was more aggressive. He put his hands to his head in shocked disbelief. Then he raced over and began yelling at Joyce. The crowd let out a chorus of boos. Over the airwaves, Detroit broadcasters Jim Price and Rod Allen expressed their amazement.

"He's out! No, he's *safe*! He is safe. He's safe at first base. *Why* is he safe? I don't understand. Could he have missed the bag? Here comes Jim Leyland. Oh my goodness!"

As Tigers manager Jim Leyland argued the call, the broadcasters cued a replay. It clearly revealed that Galarraga had caught the ball and touched first base at least a half step before Donald had made it to the bag.

"Oh my goodness! Jim Joyce!" cried Tigers broadcaster Rod Allen in shocked disbelief. "Geez, Louise!"

"What a travesty! What an absolute travesty for Armando Galarraga!" said Jim Price.

But what could Armando Galarraga do but keep on pitching? He got the final out as Trevor Crowe grounded weakly to third. His catcher, Alex Avila, gave him a consolation hug. Now, as the young pitcher walked toward the Detroit dugout, he looked down at the ground. He was no longer smiling.

"I have never been this disappointed after a Tigers win," said Jim Price.

As Armando Galarraga's teammates swarmed angrily around Jim Joyce, manager Jim Leyland trotted out of the dugout once more. This time he spoke even more heatedly to Joyce. He had already seen the replay and knew that the ump had blown the call. In a few minutes, Jim Joyce would see the replay too. When he did, the sight would knock the breath out of him.

About a half hour later, a tearful Jim Joyce did what umpires almost never do. He called Armando Galarraga over to the umpires' locker room and apologized to him. He was crying as he offered the apology. Later, Joyce faced the press.

"This isn't *a* call," he said. "This is a history call, and I kicked the s--- out of it. And there's nobody that feels worse than I do. I take pride in this job, and I kicked the s--- out of it. And I took a perfect game away from that kid who worked his butt off . . . What do I say? I thought he beat the throw. I was convinced he beat the throw, until I saw the replay . . . I just missed the d--- call. I missed it from here to the wall. It was probably the most important call of my career, and I missed it."

After watching the replay in the Tigers' clubhouse, Armando Galarraga had been bitter, but Joyce's apology changed his attitude.

"He feels really bad. He probably feels more bad than me," Galarraga told reporters. "Nobody's perfect; everybody's human," he said calmly, softly. "I understand. I give a lot of credit to the guy saying, 'Hey, I need to talk to you because I want to say I'm sorry.' That don't happen. You don't see an umpire after the game say 'I'm sorry.' He felt really bad. He didn't even shower."

The next day, Jim Joyce was umpiring at home plate. As he and the other umpires walked onto the field, everyone in Comerica Park could see that Joyce's face was red and his eyes were misty. Armando Galarraga had been appointed to present Detroit's lineup card to him. As he did so, Joyce wiped tears from his eyes. Galarraga touched him lightly on the back, as if in comradeship. In turn, Joyce patted Galarraga on the shoulder. Rather than boo Jim Joyce for the blown call, the crowd cheered. They cheered, too, when General Motors presented Galarraga with a shiny new red Chevrolet Corvette. They knew sportsmanship when they saw it.

Like Jim Joyce, Jim Leyland is a baseball veteran. As he reflected on the events of the day before, he offered this opinion: "That's the nature of the business. The players are human, the umpires are human, the managers are human, the writers are human. We all make mistakes, so that's just part of it. You just move on. It's a crying shame, but Jimmy's a real good umpire, has been for a long time. And . . . he probably got it wrong." Then he added, "This game will never be forgotten. This game will be talked about forever."

The behavior of Galarraga and Joyce inspired praise from Little League fields to the National Baseball Hall of Fame to the White House.

"Instantly, the game became a historic moment in baseball, one that has spurred interest among fans around the globe," Hall of Fame spokesman Brad Horn said. "The game's outcome shows the human element of sportsmanship, character and integrity by all parties involved, which helped the moment transcend a single feat or performance."

Today Armando Galarraga's shoes, a ball, and the first-base bag from "the perfect game that wasn't" are on display in the National Baseball Hall of Fame in Cooperstown, New York. The grace and good sportsmanship Galarraga showed in forgiving Jim Joyce have given him a more important place in baseball history than if the umpire had called Jason Donald out.

About the Book

Few of us can sink a three-point jump shot, hit a blazing fastball, or throw a sixty-yard touchdown pass. Yet we can all gain inspiration from those who perform such feats. In *Great Moments in Sports*, we witness situations in which great athletes defy the odds and emerge victorious. The incredible achievements of such athletes lead us to think, "If they can do it, maybe so can I." So performing well under pressure is one theme that runs through the book.

Another theme that runs through *Great Moments* is that of breaking down barriers. Throughout American history, minority groups have used sports to break down social and economic barriers. In boxing, Joe Louis proved that a black heavyweight could be a popular champion. In baseball, Jackie Robinson withstood racist insults and broke a color barrier that had existed for fifty years. By so doing, he helped open other fields to blacks. Similarly, Roberto Clemente overcame prejudice to become Major League Baseball's first Latino superstar. By proving himself a great player as well as a man of the people, he helped pave the way for Latinos to enter the American mainstream. In basketball, Michael Jordan proved that a black superstar could sell millions of dollars' worth of sports merchandise to white America. As a result, he helped other black stars gain a greater share of the profits from pro sports.

The stories in *Great Moments in Sports* also show us what it takes to overcome obstacles. Sometimes the obstacles athletes face are self-created, as in the case of Joe Louis. Before he faced Max Schmeling for the first time, Louis was cocky and overconfident. As a result, he didn't train as hard as he should have. But after Schmeling knocked him out, Louis recognized that the reason he had lost was his own lack of effort. After once again dedicating himself to training, Louis knocked out Schmeling in the first round of their rematch.

Sometimes political events challenge an athlete. Although Muhammad Ali was stripped of his title for refusing to fight in Vietnam, he did not give up. Instead, he fought back through the U.S. court system and in the ring. In 1974, he regained the world heavyweight championship by knocking out odds-on favorite George Foreman.

Sometimes high expectations can put pressure on an athlete. When the New York Giants drafted Eli Manning, sportswriters expected him to be a great quarterback like his older brother Peyton. When Eli took longer to develop, the writers called him a flop. Yet Eli continued to believe in himself. In 2009, the "flop" led the Giants to Super Bowl victory against the heavily favored New England Patriots.

Teamwork is another thread that runs through *Great Moments in Sports*. Joe Namath couldn't have defeated the Baltimore Colts without the help of his "team of rejects." Nor could Terry Bradshaw have won four Super Bowls without the help of some very talented teammates. Many believe that Michael Jordan is the greatest basketball player ever. However, the Bulls did not win a single championship until coach Phil Jackson molded them into a great team. Even boxers such as Joe Louis and Muhammad Ali have had excellent trainers on their side. "I could not have done it alone" is something that every great athlete can truthfully say.

Unfortunately, the examples sports provide are not always positive. In the late 1990s and early 2000s, sluggers Mark McGwire and Sammy Sosa began taking steroids. As a result, home-run records fell, and fans flocked to the games. Although there were rumors that some players were "juicing," baseball owners looked the other way. The only thing they seemed to care about was increased ticket sales. Not long afterward, Barry Bonds jumped on the steroids bandwagon. Pitching great Roger Clemens was also accused of using performance-enhancing drugs. Although drug testing may have reduced the number of players using steroids, the behavior of these four superstars suggests that some athletes—now and in the future—will do anything to advance their careers.

Given the enormous pressure to succeed in sports, it's refreshing when an athlete performs a simple act of kindness. In "The Perfect Game That Wasn't," Detroit right-hander Armando Galarraga pitches what appears to be a perfect game. But when first-base umpire Jim Joyce blows the last call of the game, Galarraga has to settle for a one-hitter. After Joyce views video of the play, he tearfully apologizes to Galarraga. Although very disappointed, Galarraga forgives the ump. "Nobody's perfect; everybody's human," he calmly explains. That's a lesson in sportsmanship that any fan can take to heart.

If you liked
Great Moments in Sports
you may be interested
in other stories
in the Townsend Library.

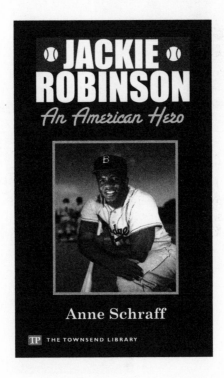

continued on the following pages

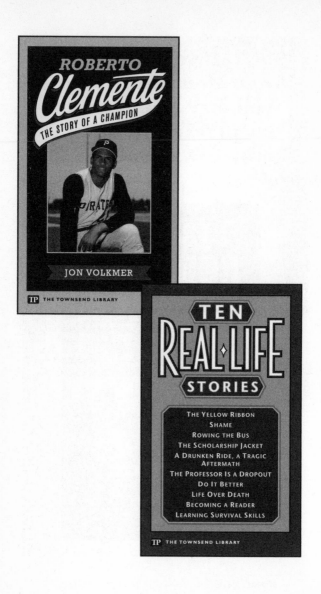

ROBERTO
Clemente
THE STORY OF A CHAMPION

JON VOLKMER

TP THE TOWNSEND LIBRARY

TEN
REAL·LIFE
STORIES

THE YELLOW RIBBON
SHAME
ROWING THE BUS
THE SCHOLARSHIP JACKET
A DRUNKEN RIDE, A TRAGIC
AFTERMATH
THE PROFESSOR IS A DROPOUT
DO IT BETTER
LIFE OVER DEATH
BECOMING A READER
LEARNING SURVIVAL SKILLS

TP THE TOWNSEND LIBRARY

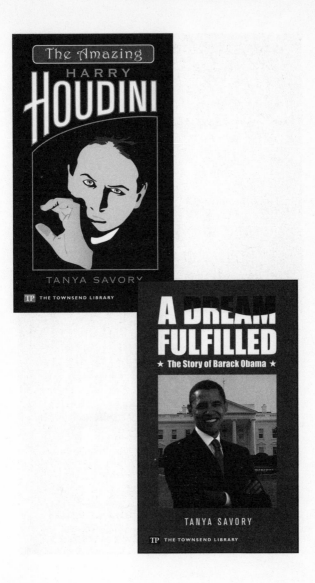